KITCHENER'S LOST BOYS

KITCHENER'S LOST BOYS

FROM THE PLAYING FIELDS TO THE KILLING FIELDS

JOHN OAKES

First published 2009

The History Press
The Mill, Brimscombe Port
Stroud, Gloucestershire, GL5 2QG
www.thehistorypress.co.uk

© John Oakes, 2009

The right of John Oakes to be identified as the Author
of this work has been asserted in accordance with the
Copyrights, Designs and Patents Act 1988.

British Library Cataloguing in Publication Data.
A catalogue record for this book is available from the British Library.

ISBN 978 0 7524 4930 2

Typesetting and origination by The History Press
Printed in Great Britain

CONTENTS

ACKNOWLEDGEMENTS

Without my wife's close and detailed scrutiny, my work would be totally unreadable. That she may have been able to rescue something of value is a tribute to her patience. To those of The History Press who have done their best to rescue the rest, including Robin Harries and Abbie Wood, I offer apologies and thanks in equal measure.

In 2002, Dr Martin Parsons and I became interested in the motivation of young officers in combat regiments during the Great War. With the enthusiastic support of Paul Holness, we gathered evidence and published the results in 2003. The work we did then has provided the basic research for this book and my debt to Martin and Paul is, I hope, repaid herein.

Chris Widdows of the Old Redingensians, and late of the Honourable Artillery Company, has been patient and generous with his time, especially in the search for illustrations. Ken Brown, the archivist of the Old Redingensians Association, is also due many thanks.

The Principal and his staff at Reading School have generously allowed me free access to the school library and archives. It will be obvious that my debt to *The Times* archive is enormous. These two sources have provided much of the primary evidence on which this book is based. Lt. Colonel Leslie Wilson of the Queen's Royal Surrey Regiment Association has given me permission to publish the valuable letter written by Edward Dwyer VC.

I have benefited from the kind advice of a number of people. Amongst them are the historians Ned Holt and Peter Hurst, and the horseman, Peter Cox. It was Sophie Bradshaw's idea which has evolved into this book.

FOREWORD

by Lt Col (Retired) Neale Jouques, OBE

The British Joint Services Command and Staff College is housed in a striking purpose-built building at Watchfield, near Swindon. It has combined the higher command and staff training schools of the three military Services with training for MoD civil servants and foreign students from military forces across the Globe. I was privileged to attend as one of the first students of the new college in 2001. The modern construction is based around a vast circular atrium and stretching out east and west of this core is a long, spine-like corridor, some three storeys high, from which the various lecture theatres, syndicate rooms and accommodation are found. The many inspiring and traditional military paintings inherited from the individual Service colleges would have been lost in such a cavernous space and so the decision was taken to fill the blank walls with a dozen vast prints taken from military photographs of the last one hundred years.

The scale and setting of these images rendered them even more striking and even those views that I had seen before gained a new impact, but one image always drew my eye as I walked past it every day and has remained indelibly etched in my mind since then. It was of a group of soldiers from a Scottish regiment, huddled together against the backdrop of the battlefield of the Western Front. Their demeanour, equipment, shrouded kilts and the grim setting exuded a resolute weariness but somehow the image and emotion captured in each magnified face tells more; a tableau of hope, humour, humanity, comradeship and determination. As a modern soldier I have always been fascinated by the First World War, not for the tales of dramatic battles but in admiration of the individuals who endured the trials of the trenches. Unlike any other episode in Britain's military past, cinema, literature and historical study have focused on the human tragedy of the 'war to end all wars.' It is embodied in the annual Poppy Appeal, albeit that over time pathos has seemed to subsume the important element of learning from what has gone before, and the populist view of 'lions led by donkeys.' I have always been somewhat sceptical of such absolute assertions. Certainly there were some poor commanders – just as there have been in many conflicts before and after the First World War – but equally there were many brave and effective ones. I also look to the attrition inflicted on Allied Forces in the journey from Normandy and Kursk to Berlin as evidence that this was not the only example in history of total war and its human cost.

But what has intrigued me the most about the 1914–18 war are the motivations and qualities of the soldiers who participated – personified by those twenty or so faces on the wall of the Staff College. The suggestion that so many thousands were collectively duped or had somehow sleep-walked into Armageddon has always struck me as an insult to the memory of our forbears. Certainly, they were living in a society that had become accustomed to British Forces being engaged in conflicts across the World and the realities associated with participation. These were people with hopes like any of us, who were prepared to forsake their livelihoods and aspirations for a greater good.

Perhaps in the modern age of the individual, such a concept might appear somewhat alien, and the passage of time means that the survivors of the First World War are sadly dwindling. Their firsthand accounts have always been modest and matter-of-fact, which has only served to stimulate my interest. How could such men steel themselves for the rigours of trench life, to be placed in harm's way time and again and cope with the loss of so many comrades?

I have served in every conflict area the British Army has been engaged in over the last twenty years, most of which have been policing-type roles with only fleeting and abstract threats and experiences. It was not really until 2006 in Helmand Province, Afghanistan, that I came even close to the insight that had eluded me previously of what drove those troops in Flanders. As we now witness in the media, the British Army is engaged in a challenging and protracted counter-insurgency warfare of an intensity not experienced since the Korean War. Daily, servicemen and women play a cat-and-mouse game with the Taleban, witness the loss of comrades, enter areas in the knowledge from electronic chatter that the enemy is preparing to attack, and return to areas where friends have fallen. Their efforts have drawn support and admiration from a public unused to the hardships of war, yet what sustains them is not the knowledge of what is going on back at home or some false bravado that, if it exists at all, is extinguished in the first contact. It is a sense of duty, comradeship and the stoicism that has prevailed on many a foreign field throughout history. In that sense, I believe we have a new-found affinity with those faces from the trenches and can relate to them as individuals. Equally, I have come to believe that we are not so far removed from them as we might think or be led to believe; those values and qualities displayed by past and present soldiers alike, however publicly unfashionable, still course through our culture.

I first met John Oakes when he taught me Biology in my second year at Reading School. The initial impression he gave was of a somewhat severe and distant soul but over time it was evident that he was passionate about his subject, the development of the boys he taught and the school itself. He was fiercely loyal, rightly proud of his Service past and tempered that initial impression with humility and good humour. In a sense he was the absolute embodiment of a school that for 800 years had championed education, character and principles in anyone fortunate to become a pupil. It was the late 1970s and grammar schools – and I suspect many of the teachers working within them – were regarded as something of an anachronism. Yet he, and the School, remained true to its values and do so still today. This is why it seems so entirely apt that John should have prepared a book on pupils past and their experiences in the First World War. In so doing he has brought them alive as individuals, as team members, added colour to the images of those times and paid homage to their motivations and selflessness. His painstaking research and accounts of real people serves as a telling reminder of the human aspect of the First World War, even as it fades further into history, and a reference point for the corresponding attributes illustrated by members of our Armed Forces today.

INTRODUCTION

They send some funny people over here nowadays.
I hope we are lucky and get a youngster straight from school.
They're the kind that do the best.

Osborne, speculating about a new officer in March 1918 (quoted in R.C. Sherriff, *Journey's End.*)

There were well over 250,000 underage soldiers in Kitchener's new armies during the First World War. In the early stages of the war, numerous young men left their public schools and were granted commissions in the army. Required to lead their men from the front, a disproportionate number of these young officers were killed or wounded. Thousands of them suffered from shell-shock. Many fought brilliantly and gained gallantry awards. Some of their stories are recounted in this book.

Why were they there? As usual, the simple question produces numerous answers which pose more questions. These lead into the special nature of male adolescence, the prevailing state of public opinion, the pay rates of recruiting sergeants, the efficiency of examining medical officers, the overwhelming rush of volunteers during the first months of the war and the confusion surrounding the first efforts to accommodate and train them.

In the course of investigating these matters, it became clear that there was a long history of recruiting very young men into the British Army. What is more, there had been a similar recruitment of adolescent men into the Imperial Yeomanry during the Boer War. This was an uncanny precursor to the recruiting shambles which occurred during the opening months of the First World War. As far as I am aware, no one has yet examined this connection.

Why were the underage recruits not found and sent home? Firstly, they had lied about their age and their relative youth may not have been easy to spot. Many young officers were only in their teens anyway. There are other reasons, some of which have to do with the huge bureaucratic machine which supported the army at war.

The British people embarked on the First World War imbued with an imperial vision tempered by Edwardian liberalism. The army was still largely Victorian in outlook. The necessary reforms to its command structure had only been in place for a few years and its most recent combat experience had been gained in the Boer War. In fact, the principal commanders in the early stages of the war – French, Haig and Hamilton, for example – had come to prominence during the great cavalry actions in the South African *veldt*. The chief of the Imperial General Staff, Lord Robertson – the man charged with converting the government's will into military action – had himself been an underage recruit. He, too, had practised his staff work in the Boer War.

Mass volunteering for Kitchener's new armies was possible because there was a set of conditions in Britain, including the presence of Lord Kitchener himself, which had not existed before and will never be repeated. A significant number of the British people, like their prime minister, H.H. Asquith, were under the delusion that they could win the war and carry on with business as usual. Imbued with imperial ideology and not hitherto challenged with any force, the British were shocked by the opposition that their war in South Africa had engendered and resented the German Kaiser's political and military support for the Boer republics. From this point onwards, the taint of paranoia infected the collective British mindset and it became pronounced in the summer of 1914. A naval arms race, instigated by the Germans to threaten British sea power, had increased the developing 'Germanophobia'.

There was a general ignorance of the maintenance and management of mass armies and a lack of industrial preparation for the modern war which was to emerge. The British had always won their wars, but against inferior opposition. They looked upon the German Army as laughable. New army recruits were surprised when they received their first induction into trench warfare to be told the Fritz was a good soldier, not a comic opera buffoon.

The bellicose atmosphere at the time of mobilisation in 1914 was palpable. A flush of imperial optimism followed Kitchener's call for 100,000 volunteers for his New Army. Among many manifestations of patriotic fervour, some of the faded glamour of Queen Victoria's golden reign was still discernable. Some notable Boer War 'Dug Outs' emerged to try to revive one of the most famous irregular corps of the South African conflict. On 13 August 1914 they placed a notice in *The Times* which read:

> Lord Roberts and Lord Ridley have joined the Committee of the revived Imperial Light Horse, and General Sir Bindon Blood will be the selecting officer. Enrolments are being made at 3, St James's Street, S.W. Old Members of the regiment are asked to communicate with Mr. J. Fergusson at 3 Neville Street, S.W.

The Imperial Light Horse claimed a connection with the infamous Jameson Raid mounted by Cecil Rhodes' right-hand man, Dr Leander Starr Jameson. This was the quixotic and doomed raid which so spectacularly failed to achieve a coup in the Boer Republic of the Transvaal in January 1896. The idea that a number of ex-colonial mounted infantrymen would dash out to Belgium to face the might of the German Army in 1914 is ludicrous in hindsight, but the advert was serious enough and Lord Roberts was one of Asquith's early military advisors.

There is a contemporary picture which illustrates the point for us. Each year on the monarch's official birthday, the ceremony of Trooping the Colour takes place on Horse Guards Parade. The Foot Guards, dressed in uniforms designed in the Victorian era, execute drills evolved to manoeuvre large bodies of disciplined soldiers to deliver volleys of musket balls. The cavalry regiments manoeuvre their horses at the walk and the trot in formations which were appropriate for the Charge of the

Light Brigade in the Crimean War. The King's Troop of the Royal Horse Artillery trots past the monarch on its superb horses towing obselete but much-revered guns. The monarch's lesser family watches the military pageant from the old commander-in-chief's room in Horseguards, the antiquated warren of offices which used to be the army's headquarters in Victorian times.

Officers from foreign armies and diplomats from strange governments are permitted to watch and admire from stands close to the monarch. It is only after the great parade is over and the ordinary people join in the procession up the Mall to Buckingham Palace that the Royal Air Force, formed at the very end of the First World War, flies over The Mall in the hugely expensive aircraft of the modern war which can deliver bombs with pinpoint accuracy. The contrast is enormous.

It was the Victorian army, as exemplified by the ceremony of Trooping the Colour, that the Lost Boys joined. It had always recruited its best soldiers when they were teenagers. It saw no reason to change its ways, until the old army died in the Ypres Salient and the terrors of modern warfare came home to haunt the British people. The Victorian army was left behind and the modern army, more akin to that which takes the field of battle today, was born. It was realised that the trenches were no place for boys to be but it was too late. There were not enough men left and a conscript army was filled up with lads of eighteen who had been fished out of their homes to fight the last battles of the war. It was at this stage that a large number of boys, too young and naive to fight, were dragooned into the trenches.

This book examines reasons why young men volunteered in droves to fight the Germans and how they trained and were transported to the front. By means of their letters, we are able to get into their way of thinking and experience a little of their life in combat – and the after-effects on their minds. Some of the myths which have grown up around them are examined briefly, as is the tardy way they were demobilised. Finally, the prospects they faced when they got home are given some thought because it was not a land fit for heroes to which they returned.

1

THE SACRIFICIAL
SCHOOLBOY

But youth's fair form, though fallen, is ever fair,
And beautiful in death the boy appears,
The hero boy, that dies in blooming years;
In man's regrets he lives, and woman's tears,
More sacred than in life, and lovelier far,
For having perished in the front of war.

Tyrtacus c.600 BC.
Translated by Thomas Campbell (1777–1844).

'Rupert Brooke is dead' wrote Winston Churchill in a brilliant obituary appearing in *The Times* on Wednesday 26 April 1915.

A telegram from the Admiral at Lemnos tells us that his life has been closed at the moment when it seemed to have reached its springtime. A voice had become audible, a note had been struck, more true, more thrilling, more able to do justice to the nobility of our youth in arms engaged in the present war than any other – more able to express their thoughts of self surrender, and with a power to carry comfort to those who watch them so intently from afar. The voice has been swiftly stilled. Only the echoes and the memory remain; but they will linger.

During the last few months of his life, months of preparation in gallant comradeship and open air, the poet soldier told with all the simple force of genius, the sorrow of youth about to die, and the sure triumphant consolations of a sincere and valiant spirit. He expected to die: he was willing to die for the dear England whose beauty and majesty he knew; and he advanced towards the brink in perfect serenity, with the absolute conviction of the rightness of his country's cause and a heart devoid of hate for his fellow men.

The thoughts to which he gave expression in the very few incomparable war sonnets he left behind will be shared by many thousands of young men moving resolutely and blithely forward into this, the hardest, the cruellest, the least-rewarding of all the wars that men have fought.

No doubt Churchill was genuinely saddened by Brooke's death but there is room to suspect that he had a further motive for writing so movingly about a young officer at the time of the Gallipoli landings. He had led the faction in government which had proposed the attack on the Turks, who had entered the war on the side of Germany and the Central Powers. It was a tremendous gamble. The strategic objective was the Turkish capital of Constantinople, the city which commanded the links between Europe, Asia, the Black Sea and the Mediterranean. The objective was to be achieved by an amphibious landing on the beaches of the Gallipoli Peninsula, which dominated the Dardanelle Straits leading to the Sea of Marmora and the Bosphorus.

Churchill's eulogy helped to establish the myth of youth, which was growing around Rupert Brooke. It was also, in modern terms, a spin doctor's coup. It moved the propaganda war forward by glorifying the notion that it was good and right for the young to die for their country. The influence held by novels, boys' own papers, popular songs, films, posters, cigarette cards, postcards, school books and commercial advertising over adolescent minds in the years preceding the First World War is worth further exploration.

The power of poetry used in the manipulation of public opinion at that time cannot be overlooked. Poetry and fiction had a disproportionate effect, by feeding the imaginative appetites of its readers. It had an emotional and long-lasting impact by becoming incorporated in its reader's inner personal narrative. It was hard to escape its effect without conscious intellectual effort and most people were not intellectuals and had other things to do anyway. The popular poets and writers of juvenile literature, by validating the imperial warrior hero, helped to mobilise public consent for the declaration of war and for the recruitment of boys into the army.

The government was aware of the power of prominent authors and harnessed it once war had commenced. Kipling was one of several writers who joined the War Propaganda Unit (WPU) set up on 2 September 1914 by the Liberal MP, Charles Masterman, at the behest of David Lloyd George, then chancellor of the exchequer. Kipling wrote a small booklet for the unit entitled *The New Army in Training*, which will be discussed later. Kipling was just one of a number of prominent authors who lent their services to the war effort. Masterman persuaded Arthur Conan Doyle, John Masefield, G.K. Chesterton, Hilaire Belloc and John Buchan, among others, to write for him. In all, the War Propaganda Unit published 1,160 pamphlets. Though the WPU may have been an effective propaganda arm during the war, no such organisation existed before hostilities commenced. (Many prominent men, not just Kipling and his fellow authors, actively supported the war; they gave money to raise regiments, made speeches at recruiting drives and even gave up their houses as billets.)

Rupert Brooke has been called a war poet. This is a misnomer. He was a before-the-war poet and his influence on the recruitment of public opinion and on the youth culture of the day was significant. His rise to fame is worth charting.

In September 1914 Churchill, then First Lord of the Admiralty, was persuaded to use his influence and obtained a commission for Brooke in the Royal Naval Division, which was to be despatched with the British Expeditionary Force to France. In the event, the RND was diverted to Belgium following an offensive by the Germans, led by General von Bosler, on 28 September 1914. Von Bosler's force of five divisions, with its 173 guns, began firing upon the outer south-east forts defending the city and port of Antwerp. The British cabinet was greatly concerned; if Antwerp was captured by the Germans, they might be able to take the French channel ports, making it near impossible to land British troops and supplies for the war in France and Belgium. Consequently, the British government decided to send a division of troops to assist in the defence of the city.

On 2 October the Germans penetrated two of Antwerp's forts, and Churchill was sent to the city to report on the situation in person. Leaving London that night, he spent three days inspecting the fortifications around the city. He reported to Kitchener on 4 October that Belgian resistance was weakening, and Kitchener despatched the British relief force to Belgium. Landing at Ostend on 6 October, it was too late to save Antwerp. The city was evacuated the following day and its Belgian military governor formally surrendered on 10 October. The British intervention prolonged the defence of Antwerp for a few days and Rupert Brooke was a participant in one of the first British engagements of the First World War.

After Antwerp, Brooke wrote of his passion for war in an explicitly youth-oriented sequence of sonnets which he called '1914'. They were a call to arms for his generation and they articulated sentiments held by a significant number of young male adolescents. One stanza of his sonnet, 'The Dead', glamorised the sacrificial schoolboy and had a disproportionate effect on the mobilisation of consent, a key factor in the manipulation of public opinion:

> Blow out, you bugles, over the rich Dead!
> There's none of these so lonely and poor of old,
> But, dying, has made us rarer gifts than gold.
> These laid the worlds away; poured out the red
> Sweet wine of youth; gave up the years to be
> Of work and joy, and that unhoped serene,
> That man calls age; and those who would have been
> Their sons, they gave their immortality.

On St George's Day, 23 April 1915, Rupert Brooke died of blood poisoning resulting from a mosquito bite while on his way with the Royal Naval Division's Hood Battalion to take part in the Gallipoli landings. Dean Inge read out one of his sonnets, 'The Soldier', from the pulpit of St Paul's cathedral on Easter Sunday 1915:

> If I should die, think only this of me:
> That there's some corner of a foreign field
> That is forever England. There shall be
> In that rich earth a richer dust concealed;
> A dust whom England bore, shaped, made aware,

Gave, once, her flowers of love, her ways to roam,
A body of England's, breathing English air,
Washed by rivers, blest by suns of home.

And think, this heart, all evil shed away,
A pulse in the eternal mind, no less
Gives somewhere back the thoughts by England given;
Her sights and sounds; dreams happy as her day;
And laughter, learnt of friends; and gentleness,
In hearts at peace, under an English heaven.

This was no new concept arising out of Brooke's poems and Churchill's intervention but, like all effective propaganda, it exploited and legitimised a widely-held sentiment. It is easy to find it exhibited in the obituaries of too many boy soldiers. Here are some of those published in the Roll of Honour in *The Times*.

> Second Lieutenant Dudley Hurst-Brown, R.F.A., who died on June 15th from wounds received the same day in Flanders, was 18 years old on June 8, ... He was educated at Cardwalles, Maidenhead, and Winchester, where he was in the O.T.C., and it was his intention upon leaving Winchester in the autumn of this year to proceed to Oxford and enter the Army through the University, the same as his elder brother, but, war breaking out, he immediately offered his services and received his commission in the Special Reserve on August 11, 1914. He was at the front for five months, during which time he went through some of the most severe fighting, but escaped injury until receiving his fatal wound. In his letter received the day before his death he stated how glad he was to be at the front, although the fighting was becoming frightful and that he saw little chance as a junior officer of ever getting safely home again, and concluded the letter with the famous Latin epitaph of Horace, 'Dulce et decorum est pro patria mori'.

Dudley Hurst-Brown had left his schoolroom to fight at the age of seventeen. He knew he would die but was motivated by the prospect of honourable sacrifice.

A further search at random among the obituaries in *The Times* for July 1916 all too easily reveals boys who went straight from school into the army and thence to the killing fields. In common with Dudley

Hurst-Brown, they were often public schoolboys who had been in the Officer Training Corps:

Lieutenant Alexander James Begg, Highland Light Infantry, who died on July 10 of wounds received on July 1 ... he was awarded the Military Cross for conspicuous bravery in organising and carrying out a successful raid on the German trenches in April, when he was wounded. Educated at Glasgow Academy and Fettes College, he played in the football team and the fives team, and was a cadet sergeant in the O.T.C. He received his commission on leaving school in September 1915.

Lieutenant James Stanley Lightfoot Welch. Yorkshire Light Infantry ... educated at the Preparatory School of Upper Canada College, Toronto and Yardley Court, Tonbridge, and at Rugby where he was a member of the O.T.C., and a scholar. In 1913 he was elected to an open scholarship at King's College, Cambridge, and would have gone up to Cambridge in October 1914. When war broke out he applied for a commission, and was gazetted in October 1914, being promoted the following May. A letter from his commanding officer says that whilst he was leading his platoon against the enemy he was first wounded by a bullet and fell, but was immediately afterward killed by a shell. His last words to his platoon were *Never mind me – carry on.*

The Times, 13 July 1916.

A few days later and the following obituary appeared:

Second Lieutenant J. Victor Sinnet-Jones, Royal Welsh Fusiliers, who fell last week in France ... was educated at Llandaff Choir School and at King's School, Worcester, where he was prominent in work and games. He obtained a temporary commission from the School O.T.C. in August last instead of going to Oxford to prepare for holy orders. His elder brother in the same regiment fell earlier in the war.

The Times, 27 July 1916.

That these schoolboy soldiers and many others like them died in July 1916 is no surprise; that was the first month of the deadly Battle of the Somme. An offensive was launched with the aim of making a breakthrough in the German lines for a cavalry attack. The infantry offensive was preceded by a great deal of artillery work. The tasks the gunners undertook were varied. They were required to interrupt the work of the German staff, disrupt their supply lines, knock out their artillery and break their communications systems and, as far as possible, destroy their front line fortifications and make gaps in the barbed wire. They also needed to kill or incapacitate German troops and reduce the morale of the survivors. The Germans were particularly rich in machine guns which they had sited with care and protected well to resist the best efforts of the British artillery. It takes a great deal of time to train gunners properly. That was a luxury the New Army volunteers lacked but, even so, they gave a good account of themselves. At dawn on 1 July 1916, following an intensive 'shock and awe' artillery barrage on the German fortifications, the Allies attacked along a twenty-five mile front. The British troops, who were funnelling through gaps in their own wire, were mown down by withering fire from the numerous German machine guns, which were sited to aim at their legs and lower bodies.

On the first day the British lost around 1,000 officers and 19,240 men. The battle continued until 18 November, by which time approximately 95,675 British were dead. These figures must be viewed with some caution, however, because there were not enough clerks in the British Army to compile accurate statistics.

Kitchener's New Army took the brunt of it all but it must be remembered that it was fighting German veterans who were well protected in cavernous strongholds dug in chalk. Against all precedents and expectations, there were very few British stragglers. Shells and streams of machine-gun bullets made gaps in the lines of khaki figures but the survivors continued to surge forward with dogged determination. Only well-led and well-motivated men could have survived such an ordeal without breaking. The men of the New Army entered the Somme as sporting athletes and emerged as cautious professional soldiers.

The proportion of young subalterns who were killed, wounded or hospitalised with shell-shock was inordinately high. They led their men in battle and that required extraordinary courage, which must have been the fruit of intense indoctrination. In the early years of the war the similarity of their education is striking. They were mostly ex-public schoolboys who had been members of the Officer Training Corps. It is no surprise to find that 516 Old Harrovians were killed in the First World War, approximately one every three days.

The lowest age for the recruitment of officers during the First World War was officially seventeen years and six months and a good number of them were killed before they were eighteen. They were, of course, adolescents and particularly vulnerable to propaganda. The term adolescent was not in regular use in 1914 but it serves well enough to describe that period between childhood and adulthood, through which the human animal must, perforce, pass. In some societies there are initiation ceremonies to mark developmental changes. In modern Britain there is a heavier emphasis on this period than there was in the early twentieth century but there is every reason to believe that the developmental changes took place then as now, though with some emphasised and others muted by the impact of different environments.

The human brain develops to cope with the physiological changes taking place during adolescence. The parts controlling all the other regions shift during this time. In the words of Professor Nicholas Allen of Melbourne University: 'Your 6ft 2in son can manage some very complicated work yet still does dumb things.' In fact, his brain is still developing and will go on doing so until he is around twenty.

Adolescence is a period in which self-image is very important. Young people are constantly focusing on the reaction of what we now call significant others, such as friends, family members, role models and leading personalities. They will try to adopt styles of behaviour or appearance which conform to the ideal of the moment. This was particularly significant at the time of signing up for military service and was heavily influenced by the imperialist ideology and hero cult prevalent in 1914.

Adolescents can be persuaded to search for identity in a destructive way, by being cruel and intolerant towards people who are different to themselves in ethnicity, nationality and mode of dress. Thus they can be influenced by propaganda to focus their intolerance on another race or people and to resort to violence or take up arms against them. In 1914 the German was represented as the 'Despicable Hun' who murdered Belgian women and children and who aspired to invade Britain and curtail her empire.

In adolescence there is a sense of invulnerability, yet to be modified by experience. In 1914 and 1915 this influenced the decision to enlist and the real dangers of war to be ignored or, at least, overlooked. It is that sense of invulnerability which now contributes to the number of temporary roadside shrines, so common on British roads, marking the places where young men have killed themselves and often their passengers by driving recklessly.

They are opportunists. The dream of returning home, secure in proven manhood, immunised by gallantry medals and heroic scars from the criticism of parents, peers, teachers, employers and rivals, and the prospect of compliant feminine attention, led quickly and directly to the recruiting office. The adolescent tendency to act impulsively is illustrated in the case of sixteen-year-old east Londoner, H. Sullivan, who enlisted in June 1915. He wrote:

> I was looking at some Army posters in Commercial Road. A recruiting
> sergeant tapped me on the shoulder. 'What about it mate? Like to join?' –
> I was about to say I am only sixteen, changed my mind ... thought here's
> a lark! I said, 'Yes mate, if I'm big enough!'

He joined the Shoreditch Battalion (20th Middlesex Regiment). Another sixteen-year-old, Alfred Allen, was so infatuated with the bands patrolling the streets of Brighton that he volunteered at his local drill hall. George Coppard was only sixteen when he was so roused by the news placards at every street corner and the military bands blaring out martial music that he could not resist volunteering. (All three quoted from Simkins, Chapter 6.) The analysis of adolescence is derived from my own experience as a House Master who lived under the same roof as forty-five boys between the ages of eleven and nineteen for ten years. Since practical experience is rarely accepted over the opinions of experts, I have severely paraphrased the work of Erik H. Erikson in his *Adolescence et crise: la quête de l'identité*, (Flammeron, Paris, 1972).

On 27 June 1944 Herbert Hoover, sometime President of the United States of America, reminded his audience that 'Older men declare war. But it is youth that must fight and die.' After the Great War, aged politicians were criticised for their role in sending young boys to the front to be killed or maimed. One provocative view, that of Gunnar Heinshon in his book *Shöne und Weitmacht*, is that societies with a high population of young men are apt to resort to violence to solve political or ideological problems.

Heinshon argues that in these societies there are not enough positions to provide all the young men with status. Becoming a military hero offers a way for younger male siblings to gain approval. He also argues that societies in which large families are common are more likely to go to war than those with small families. The fewer children per family, the less expendable they become. He goes on to suggest that when fifteen to twenty-nine year olds make up more than thirty per cent of the population, violence is more likely to be used to resolve disputes. Germany's nationalism during the First World War may be explained in this way.[1] In the light of these assertions it is interesting to note that England's population grew from 15.91 million in 1841 to 36.07 million in 1911 and that women were not able to vote in general elections until after the war.[2]

In early twentieth-century Britain, where large families and primogeniture prevailed, the army provided a career for the younger sons of upper-class families. Most upper and many middle-class boys were sent away to boarding school at the age of eight and lived in male communities for most of their early lives. They were prepared for war and indoctrinated with an aggressive imperialist ideology by zealous school masters. Juvenile literature, as we will see later, encouraged adolescent warlike tendencies. Britain in 1914 would seem to have borne out Heinshon's hypotheses.

That there were a large number of underage soldiers in the army during the First World War is undisputed. The minimum age for voluntary service was nineteen for private soldiers. This means that every underage recruit who joined as a private solider declared his age as nineteen on his attestation form. My own rough estimate of how many boys there were is based on counting the number of boys of eighteen and under and also of nineteen and underrecorded on the memorial rolls compiled by two schools.

Out of the 523 entries where the true age of the soldier is recorded on the memorial roll made by Friends School, Lisburn, 4.8 per cent of the dead were under eighteen. From the same memorial list 10.5 per cent of the men were nineteen and under when they were killed. From the Reading School memorial list the figure for those of eighteen and under was 3.5 per cent. From the same list, 14.1 per cent were nineteen and under. The average of the two figures for the eighteen and under group is 4.15 per cent and for the nineteen and under group is 12.3 per cent.

According to a grave count made at Tyne Cot Cemetery, nearly twenty per cent of those headstones on which the official age of the soldier was engraved commemorated boys of twenty and younger.

The United Kingdom's total war dead was in the region of 908,371. Based on the two school samples, that would give a total of 37,697 who were eighteen or under when they died and 111,730 who were nineteen or under. The number of men mobilised during the war was 8,904,467. The ratio of dead to mobilised is about 1: 9.8. This would give us a very rough estimate of 360,000 young men aged eighteen or under and over 1,000,000 aged nineteen or under who were in the army during the First World War. Richard Van Emden, who is the most likely to be accurate, first estimated that 250,000 boy soldiers served in the Great War. He has since made it clear that he believes the figure is higher. As time passes we may arrive at a better estimate.

Were boy soldiers unique to the First World War? Apparently not. In *The Times* dated 24 April 1901, someone, calling himself Reform was writing about soldiers' pay at the time of the Boer War. Part of his letter reads:

> As no attempt is made to ascertain the real age of a recruit and as children of 14, 15 and 16 are enlisted, it is impossible to arrive at a just average. That average is probably well under 18 on enlistment, and when the soldier becomes officially 20 and therefore available for service in any climate he is frequently under 19.

The writer goes on to estimate that 40,000 recruits were annually enlisted at the age of eighteen and states: 'how many soldiers under 20 sent to the seat of war we will never know.'

Reform's views are reinforced in the following undated letter written by drummer John Hammond, Royal Berkshire Regiment, who was less than pleased that his battalion was stationed on the Isle of Wight during the Boer War:

> Well, in the first place, I am happy in my regiment. I have been appointed effective drummer, and now I clear 9½ d a day pay which I think very good for a boy of 15, don't you?
>
> Also my regiment feels it very keenly that we are not being sent to the war in South Africa. I think it a shame, as the 1st Royal Berks

distinguished themselves at Tofrek, on the 22nd March, 1885, and were made a royal regiment on the field of battle. I am sure we should give a good account of ourselves in South Africa if we only had the chance to go. As it is, they are bringing the Royal Sussex Regiment from Malta preparatory to sending them to South Africa, and sending us to Malta to linger in obscurity.

We have one consolation, however. There is a rumour that the Abyssinians intend overrunning the Soudan, so if we are at Malta we may have a chance at them. I am sure Menelik will find the men he can't lick in my regiment.

Thomsett is getting on well. He is also an effective drummer. All our old boys are getting on famously. We are going to have our photo taken in Khaki and I will send you one as soon as I can.

Well, I think this is all now. I hope my next letter will be from the front, either South Africa, Kruger or Menelik, it don't matter which.

John Hammond had a command of English which would not have been common among soldiers at that time. His letter is quoted in A.H. Cockerill's book *Sons of the Brave*, which is primarily about old boys of the Duke of York's Military School. Founded in 1803, it still specialises in educating soldiers' sons and daughters. John may have been a Dukie.

Cockerill also quotes a letter which he received from John Holland who had been a pupil at the Royal Hibernian School, the Irish equivalent of the Duke of York's School. In 1902 Holland was fourteen years old when he enlisted in the 91st Foot in Dublin. He writes:

> Our turn came for India very early in 1903. We had a month's leave first, then 18 of us, five sergeants, five boys and eight men, left on the troopship Sardinia. The ship also had many warriors going to Sudan, Egypt and South Africa … We reached Bombay at last and, as the harbour was so shallow, we were landed by barges. A short time later a few of us, all strangers to each other, lined up at the bar. I was last in the queue and because every one said the one behind them was paying I was caught to pay it all …

Cockerill, who studied the history of the Duke of York's School and the Royal Hibernian School extensively, concluded that these institutions produced boys who constituted the army's preferential stock and provided the army with its NCO core. His records show that there were 1,640 ex-pupils of the Duke of York's School serving in the army in 1900, of which 258 were boy soldiers who had gone directly from school into the army.

In 1914 the British people had gone to war in a mood of happy optimism. They had answered the call to arms in their droves and the volunteer soldiers, drawn from all the classes and corners of the land, had marched guilelessly to war. No other country could have raised and trained so many volunteers and the mood and the response was echoed throughout the British Empire. Of the 25 million people of the so-called White Empire, 857,000 served in the war and 141,000 were killed. India provided 1.5 million men to fight in Europe, Mesopotamia and elsewhere. By the end of it all, the British Empire was the world superpower, with the largest fleet of warships, the largest air force and the largest army. Somehow, however, everything had changed. The glory, the sense of superiority, the conviction and the certainty had been drowned in the putrid mud of the killing fields in Flanders. This haunting little poem by Siegfried Sassoon shows the awful contrast between the reality in the trenches and the war fever in Britain:

I knew a simple soldier boy
Who grinned at life in empty joy,
Slept soundly through the lonesome dark,
And whistled early with the lark.

In winter trenches, cowed and glum,
With crumps and lice and lack of rum,
He put a bullet through his brain.
No one spoke of him again.

You smug-faced crowds with kindling eye
Who cheer when soldier lads march by,
Sneak home and pray you never know
The hell where youth and laughter go.

Rudyard Kipling, the imperial poet, had lost his eighteen-year-old son Jack in the Battle of Loos. This was the battle in which eighty per cent of the British attacking force was killed or wounded and it was said that here chivalry disappeared to give way to the new tempo of battle and the rule of the machine. It was also the battle which made the British government painfully aware that voluntary recruiting alone would not supply replacements for the dead and wounded in this new type of warfare and that conscription would be necessary.

The men who survived aged rapidly and many succumbed to shell-shock. Robert Graves wrote that officers were at their best having spent three or four weeks at the front, after which neurasthenia set in, and that those between the ages of twenty-three and thirty-three could count on a longer useful life than those older or younger. Oakes and Parsons, who studied the relationship between age and death rate and rank and death rate for old boys of Reading School, broadly support Graves' observations and they also assert that by far the most dangerous rank to hold in the British Army of the First World War was that of second lieutenant.

The imperialist ideal, which embraced the concept of patriotic sacrifice in justifiable war and which claimed support from the established church, did not survive intact in the trenches and the killing fields of the First World War. The intense and prolonged horror of trench warfare was so far in excess of any previous experience that it cast those who extolled war as liars, no matter that those who propagandised the war fervently believed what they said and were guilty only of error. To lie is to say something that is not true in a conscious effort to deceive. It was an error, though, because they could and should have learnt the lessons of the American Civil War and the Russo-Japanese war, during which there were intimations of the horrors to come. They should also have known that adolescents are easy prey to warlike propaganda and to have kept so many boys in that hell on earth is not easily understood today.

Viewed from the trench, wallowing in filth, assailed by constant danger, the intractable problems of strategy and tactics were of little importance. It made little difference to those who constantly smelt the odour of decaying bodies and saw young boys killed indiscriminately that the problems of trench warfare baffled everyone until the techniques of battlefield management and the appliance of military science were developed later in the war. To many of those who were marched into the fields of fire of German machine guns, the fault lay with the generals and their staff officers. They were seen as incompetent, indifferent, distant and bloodthirsty. After experiences like that the traditional compact between rulers and the ruled, which had been the glue which held the army together, was severely tested.

Those war poets who had entered the war imbued with patriotic fervour expressed their change of perspective through their poetry. Siegfried Sassoon wrote the intensely warlike poem 'The Kiss', in which he deliberately linked the glories of the Great War with heroic battles of the past. However, as the war progressed, he wrote in his poem 'Base Details' of how the old reverence for authority was breaking down, by satirising scarlet majors, that is majors who wore red tabs on their uniforms to show that they were on the staff:

> If I were fierce, and bald and short of breath,
> I'd live with scarlet Majors at the Base,
> And speed glum heroes up the line to death.
> You'd see me with my puffy petulant face,
> Guzzling and gulping in the best hotel,
> Reading the Roll of Honour. 'Poor young chap,'
> I'd say – 'I used to know his father well;
> Yes, we've lost heavily in this last scrap.'
> And when the war is done and youth stone dead,
> I'd toddle safely home and die – in bed.

It was true that schools, vicars, teachers, dons, poets and politicians lauded the sacrificial schoolboy and framed war in heroic terms. It is also true that many young men absorbed the story and went to war imbued with Homer's line 'Dulce et decorum est pro patria mori' deep in their psyche. Dudley Hurst-Brown, for example, wrote of it in his last letter home. It is not difficult to find Great War memorials with this line inscribed on them. One such is in Reading School Chapel. Wilfred Owen drew another conclusion in one of the most devastating of all his powerful poems:

> GAS! Gas! Quick, boys! – An ecstasy of fumbling,
> Fitting the clumsy helmets just in time;
> But someone still was yelling out and stumbling,
> And flound'ring like a man in fire or lime.
> Dim, through the misty panes and thick green light,
> As under a green sea, I saw him drowning.

In all my dreams, before my helpless sight,
He plunges at me, guttering, choking, drowning.

If in some smothering dreams you too could pace
Behind the wagon that we flung him in,
And watch the white eyes writhing in his face,
His hanging face, like a devil's sick of sin;
If you could hear, at every jolt, the blood
Come gargling from the froth-corrupted lungs,
Obscene as cancer, bitter as the cud
Of vile, incurable sores on innocent tongues,
My friend, you would not tell with such high zest
To children ardent for some desperate glory,
The old lie: Dulce et decorum est
Pro patria mori.

Whilst attacking the old lie, the war poets were aiming their shafts at the public schools and their imitators.

After the conscription of single men between the ages of eighteen and forty-one was introduced in February 1916, 2 million additional soldiers were raised, with more after May when married men were also conscripted. In July of that year the Somme offensive began, with 60,000 British casualties on the first day. By the last year of the war, Britain was running out of manpower. Therefore, age for service was expanded, both downward and upward, so that by the spring of 1918 many divisions were composed of men who might well have been at school. In the context of the sacrifice of youth, why was the fact so readily overlooked that by the winter of 1918 about half of the 1.85 million British troops serving in France and Belgium were eighteen years of age?

When the Germans, strengthened by many thousands of soldiers released from the fight with Russia, launched Operation Michael in March 1918, it was a British Army containing a large number of conscripted adolescents which bore the brunt. The German aim was to divide the French and British armies, a matter of some importance to them since the Americans had arrived in force. A total of sixty-three German divisions attacked over a sixty-mile front held by twenty-six British divisions. The attack was preceded by the most ferocious artillery bombardment of the war. The German assault finished on

5 April, by which time they had taken 90,000 British prisoners and had inflicted 164,000 casualties on the British and 70,000 on the French. Jon Savage quotes a British lance corporal who wrote about the bombardment:

> My section included four youths just turned 18 years, who had only been with our company for three weeks and whose first experience of shell fire it was and what an experience. They cried and one kept calling 'mother' and who could blame him, such hell makes weaklings of the strongest and no human nerves or body was ever built to stand such torture, noise, horror and mental pain.[3]

These were not well-fed public school volunteers hardened by years of sport and discipline. They were largely urban youths who had been malnourished, badly housed and poorly educated for much of their lives. Had the war poets written about the appalling depravation of the urban poor, they may well have had a point. They did not, and the evidence that the poor and half starved were being conscripted lies in dusty records of tedious conferences – hardly the stuff of poets but necessary for historians.

For example, on 9 July 1917, the chairman of the Parliamentary Committee, which was appointed to enquire into the conduct of medical examinations under the Military Service Acts, read out a circular written by the Deputy Director of Medical Services in the Northern Command and addressed to the presidents of the medical recruiting boards under his control. In it the Deputy Director instructed the boards to:

> understand that every man who was of any potential use whatever in the Army for fighting, marching, digging, hauling, cooking, engine driving, motor driving, or as a baker, a draughtsman, an electrician, a telegraphist and telephonist, or a member of one of the many other trades necessary for the maintenance of an army, must be placed in one category or another, and must not be lost to the army by being found permanently unfit.[4]

The boards were told to reduce their percentage of rejections to the lowest category. The same Deputy Director was later to write that, when inspecting a certain labour battalion, he was:

33

shocked to see the specimens of humanity which have been accepted as potential value to the army – men almost totally blind, deformed, of the poorest physique, men of doubtful intellect, men almost unable to stand, men with paresis which rendered locomotion almost grotesque, several cases of insanity which told their tale at a glance. This scandal must stop.

On 17 July 1917, the same committee commented that:

the Pensions Minister, Mr. Barnes, had stated in the House of Commons that 'they' had dealt with about 10,000 cases, by way of pardons and otherwise, of men who ought never to have been in the Army. The committee was quite convinced from that statement that there were many men in the Army who should not have been there.[5]

When reading the words of Private William Holmes, there can be very little surprise that he remembered two very young recruits between sixteen and seventeen years of age, who, when ordered to attack, cried their eyes out and ran away. They were, said Holmes, caught, charged with desertion, stripped of their regimental insignia and shot.[6]

For the modern Briton, the inescapable fact that the army, despite its manifest faults, won the war in the end is not as important as the dreadful losses. Somehow the last battles of the war have slipped from the public memory. As a respected teacher of history remarked recently, it is almost impossible to find a pupil who can name a battle in which the British were on the winning side. The British prefer to remember Loos, Ypres and Passchendaele. A great many young men gave their lives so that their country might defeat an enemy they saw as in the wrong. They fought at the behest of their political leaders who have, by and large, escaped the blame. It is as though the dreadful losses were for naught.

In the Court Circular published in *The Times* on 20 January 1919, a citation for the award of a Victoria Cross to a Private Thomas Ricketts appeared. It was unusual for the King's personal private secretary to include a long citation in the regular and formulaic press release of Royal comings and goings. We can assume that it was of great importance. It read:

For most conspicuous bravery and devotion to duty on the 14 October 1918, during the advance from Ledeghem, when the attack was temporally held by heavy hostile fire and the platoon to which he belonged suffered severe casualties from the fire of an enemy battery at point-blank range. He volunteered to go with his section commander and a Lewis gun to attempt to outflank the battery. Advancing in short rushes under heavy fire from enemy machine-guns, their ammunition was exhausted when still 300 yards from the battery. The enemy, seeing an opportunity to get their field guns away began to bring up their gun teams. Private Ricketts at once realising the situation, doubled back 100 yards under the heaviest machine-gun fire, procured further ammunition, dashed back again to the Lewis gun, and by very accurate fire drove the enemy and the gun teams into the farm. His platoon then advanced without casualties and captured the four field guns, four machine-guns and eight prisoners. A fifth field gun was subsequently intercepted by fire and captured.

By his presence of mind in anticipating the enemy intention and his utter disregard of personal safety, Private Ricketts secured the further supply of ammunition.

On Sunday 19 January 1919 King George V was at York Lodge, Sandringham, to where he invited a courageous boy soldier for a private investiture, having learnt that he was on his way home to Newfoundland at the end of his war service. The King was extending a special honour by presenting the Victoria Cross to a boy of seventeen in the privacy of his favourite, but modest, home in Norfolk. He made a considerable effort to entertain the boy during his visit.

The lad was given lunch in a private room before going to meet George V in the sitting room of York Lodge at 2 p.m. There the King, dressed in civilian clothes, read out the citation and pinned the VC on his tunic and they chatted for a good ten minutes. Afterwards, the young hero was taken to the gardens to meet Prince Olav of Norway, Queen Mary, Queen Alexandra, Queen Maud of Norway and Princess Victoria. The Queen Mother was moved by the occasion and pinned a rose from the garden beside the VC on the boy's breast. There will have been a number of good reasons for the King to have given personal recognition to No. 3102 Sergeant Thomas Ricketts of the 1st Battalion, Royal Newfoundland Regiment. (Ricketts had been promoted to sergeant in the field, in recognition of his outstanding bravery.) He came from Newfoundland, Britain's oldest colony, whose soldiers had fought valiantly in the last battles of war, as had the Canadians and Australians. But perhaps it was also Thomas Ricketts' extreme youth which impressed the King, who introduced him to his guests as the youngest VC in his army.

Thomas was born on 15 April 1901 at Middle Arm, White Bay, Newfoundland. He was fifteen years and four months old when he travelled to St John, where he enlisted on 2 September 1916. He shipped out to Britain on 13 January 1917. After training at Ayr, he went to France on 10 June 1917. He fought with his battalion at Cambrai, where his brother, George, was killed and on 20 November he was wounded by a bullet in the right thigh. He was evacuated to Wandsworth hospital in England and returned to France on 4 April 1918. King George V had joined the Royal Navy at the age of thirteen. Many of the midshipmen manning the boats during the Gallipoli landings in 1915 were thirteen or not much older.[7]

Mass death devastated all the belligerent armies. By the beginning of 1918, the combat soldiers were exhausted. The Russian Revolution, the French Army mutinies of 1917, the Italian defeat at Caporetto and the decline in manpower all pointed to considerable problems for the Allies. However, the British Army did not mutiny, despite the heavy losses it had sustained and despite the extreme youth of half of its soldiers. There were a number of reasons for this. Postal censorship had expanded from its original remit of security to that of scrutinising soldiers' letters for signs of disaffection. The British commanders were well aware of what made soldiers unhappy and made ready concessions to popular taste in the provision of rest and relaxation. Discipline, of course, played an important role and capital punishment was ever present as a threat. Whilst the numbers vary from source to source, the British courts martial appear to have produced 3,080 capital convictions, out of which 346 were executed. The summary nature of the courts martial can be criticised and there is a strong argument in favour of a pardon for many of those who were executed.

On the whole, the British managed their soldiers better than their allies did. Officers carefully left the application of bad language and abusive discipline to N.C.O.s and, thus, neatly remained one degree removed from the immediate problems of minor insubordination. The recognition and better treatment of shell-shock by the British hospitals did much to advance the understanding and management of behaviour under severe pressure. The British class system, though it was greatly modified in the trenches, was still a powerful controlling force. There were also rewards. The powerful incentive provided by field promotions and, especially, the distribution of gallantry awards was probably more significant than we have hitherto realised. The British were monarchists and they were motivated by the possibility that they may receive recognition from their King for gallantry in action in the form of an MC or MM. The sovereign's role in the maintenance of morale may have been more significant than many modern historians believe. That is, perhaps, why King George V was so careful to make special arrangements to invest Sergeant Ricketts with his VC and to see that the citation was carried in full in the Court Circular in *The Times*.

In the chapters which follow, arranged as they are in thematic rather than chronological order, there is an attempt to understand the recruitment of boys straight from school, their motivation and their behaviour in war.

2

WHY THEY CHOSE TO FIGHT

For all we have and are,
For all our children's fate,

Stand up and take the war,
The Hun is at the gate!

Rudyard Kipling, 'For All We Have and Are.'
The Times, 1 September 1915.

In 1940 George Orwell wrote of the First World War:

Most of the English middle class are trained for war from the cradle
onwards, not technically but morally. The earliest political slogan I can
remember is 'We want eight (dreadnoughts) and we wont wait'. At seven
years old I was a member of the Navy League and wore a sailor suit with
H.M.S. *Invincible* on my cap. Even before my public school O.T.C. I had
been in a private school cadet corps. On and off, I have been toting a rifle
ever since I was ten, in preparation not only for war but for a particular
kind of war.[1]

Some argue that the preparation for war was confined to the upper and middle classes. I suggest that it penetrated deeper into the literate working class. Orwell also wrote that 'most people are influenced far more than they would care to admit by novels, serial stories, films and so forth … from this point of view the worst books are often the most important because they are usually the ones read earliest in life.'[2]

Orwell's point is the more important because young boys, who joined Kitchener's new armies in large numbers, were influenced by what they read, heard in school, watched at the cinema and absorbed from their peers. After the Boer War, invasion stories began to take hold. Xenophobia added to the weight of imperialist propaganda and was to burst forth in a climax of anger when the Germans invaded Belgium in 1914. As a consequence there were many highly motivated young men eager to join the army in the opening months of the war. Among them there were a substantial number of boys who had yet to develop adult discernment and who were particularly vulnerable to recruitment fever. A number of factors had combined to ripen this group of adolescents for war. It only needed something to shake them off the tree. This something is known to experts in the field as the trigger.

The factors which prepared boys to fight and the triggers which led them to enlist are not without interest to those studying the present spate of violent youth crime in Britain. One example of a trigger of particular relevance to our boy soldiers is described in this passage written by J.M. Winter: 'Children stood as the images of bravery and victim-hood as far back as the Napoleonic period. But after 1914, they not only suffered, they also killed, and waited for the time when they could wreak vengeance on the enemy.' One British war poster captured the new mobilisation of children in total war. Accompanying a drawing of a devastated house a child intoned;

This is the house that Jack built.
This is the bomb that fell on the house that Jack built.
This is the Hun who dropped the bomb that fell on the house that Jack built.

This is the gun that killed the Hun who dropped the bomb that fell on the house that Jack built.

It was the child who carried the gun and intended to use it – against the Hun in his Gotha bomber or his Zeppelin, or against Huns murdering Belgian children and women.[3] Lurid stories of German atrocities in Belgium were extensively used in British propaganda to encourage recruiting, including the one about the dead German officer in whose pocket there was said to be a letter from his wife urging him to rape every foreign woman he came across.[4]

Even today there are around 300,000 children carrying arms and fighting. Injustices such as this perpetuate for years without attracting attention. This is because the victims perceive their plight as normal and are, almost by definition, inarticulate and without influence. The nineteenth-century child chimney sweeps in London and child apprentices in the cotton mills of Lancashire went un-remarked upon for years until someone was able to effect a change.

In 2004 Rachel Brett and Irma Specht published a study of adolescent volunteers in the armed forces or armed groups in Afghanistan, Columbia, Republic of Congo (Brazzaville), Republic of Congo (DRC), the United Kingdom, Sierra Leone, Sri Lanka and South Africa. They found that there were common factors which put young persons at risk of joining an armed force or armed group. In addition to the special features of adolescence, they argue that the reasons are seven in number: war; poverty; education; family and friends; culture; tradition; and ideology. All these features applied to British boys in the First World War to varying degrees, depending on the individual.

How did Brett and Specht's seven conditions apply in 1914? It seems obvious that war is a necessary precondition to the enlistment of boy soldiers. In 1914 this was certainly the case in Britain. There was suddenly a unique opportunity opened up by Kitchener's famous call to arms. It was now possible for boys to volunteer for the adventure of war. Few recruiting sergeants were checking up on the ages of recruits. In fact, there is clear evidence that it was considered normal to lie about age.

In Britain, poverty contributed greatly to underage enlistment. The growth of huge housing estates, built cheaply and badly in English manufacturing towns during the industrial revolution, had left an appalling and unique legacy of poor housing, insufficent diet, inadequate sanitation and poor health. These housing estates were a separate world, in which children's physical and social development was adversely affected. For the period 1926–9, a survey found that, at the age of thirteen, Christ's

Hospital boys were 2.4 inches taller than council schoolboys and at the age of seventeen they were 3.8 inches taller than employed males who had attended council schools.

Seebohm Rowntree described some examples of poor family living conditions in 1910 thus:

> Two rooms, seven inmates ... Dirty flock bedding in living-room placed on box and two chairs. Smell of room from dirt and bad air unbearable ... There was no water supply in the house, the eight families having to share one water tap ... with eight other families living in other houses. The grating under the water tap is used for disposal of human excreta.

Many boys volunteered to go to war in order to escape their home conditions.

What is more, the war closed many markets. Until the armament industry began to employ labour, a great number of young men were unemployed or on short-time work. One example, quoted by Peter Simkins, is that of Thomas Peers, who enlisted in August 1914 and later recalled:

> when I was a raw lad of eighteen, times were hard in my home town of Bradford and I was working three days a week and drawing three days' dole money. Idling away time one day, my friends and I were discussing the dreariness of unemployment, when someone suggested that we enlist and the Hussars were mentioned. This sounded to me a glorious adventure.[5]

Unemployment and short-time work were major and too often overlooked factors driving young men into the army. The Board of Trade figures show that unemployment rose by ten per cent in July and August 1914 and that nine out of ten men laid off had enlisted or been called up as reservists.

Education had long been neglected in England. In 1917 a Board of Education report stated that:

> public education after the Elementary School leaving age is a part-time affair. And there is very little of it. In 1911–12 there were about 2,700,000 juveniles between 14 and 18, and of these about 2,200,000 or 81.5 per cent were enrolled in neither day schools nor in evening schools.

In contrast, but nonetheless significant, public schools and their imitators started their cadet corps around the turn of the century and they also ran army sixth forms with the sole purpose of preparing pupils for the Sandhurst and Woolwich entrance exams. Such schools were incubators of imperialism.[6]

Family and friends played a unique role in recruiting for Kitchener's New Army. The introduction of Pals' Battalions meant that whole working communities could volunteer and fight together. Peter Simkins states that 'no British Army in history has contained such a high proportion of units directly linked to local communities.' It was difficult for a fit young man to avoid following his neighbours, peers or workmates into uniform. Simkins is right to emphasise this point. It is too easy to forget the localised nature of British society at the time.

School old boys' clubs and sporting clubs were very common indeed, and many were forced to close down during the war because most of their members were at the front. Their influence must not be overlooked. An example appeared in *The Times* on 4 September 1914:

> All Rugby football clubs in Kent are being asked by Mr. Rowland Hill and other old Rugby players to scratch their matches and encourage their members to join the 2nd Battalion now being raised by the 29th London (Blackheath). Clubs coming forward in sufficient numbers will form a company, or section, which will allow friends to soldier with one another. All enquiries should be addressed to … the headquarters of the Blackheath Battalion …

In 1914 Britain, culture, tradition and ideology made a unique combination. The prevailing ideology was imperialism, around which were clustered the institutions of the monarchy, parliament, the military, the church and the schools. The concept of Anglo-Saxon invincibility was paramount and the ideals of manliness, courage, pluck, character and adventure all fed on it. The perception of manliness and the position of boys in their families and society at large have changed so radically that we need to examine something of the prevailing attitudes of the early twentieth century.

Perhaps the most telling remark in this context comes from one of the stories written by the Australian author, Lillian Pyke. Many will find it offensive nowadays. In her book *Max the Sport*, she states that Max's mother is exultant with 'the triumph of one who has introduced into the world a man child … self-controlled, brave and above all innocent but not ignorant where the real truths of life are concerned.' Emphatically Max is not a 'curled darling in sashes and a petticoat but a man child and a sport.'[7]

The burden of manhood was often fatal. The fear of being seen as a coward is still a problem for male adolescents, despite the feminisation of education and popular culture. Combined with the need to impress females, it can be a powerful motivating force. In the heady atmosphere of the early days of the First World War, the particularly nasty 'Order of the White Feather' was founded by a retired admiral. He encouraged young women to seek out young males who were in civilian clothes, or whom they knew to be slow to volunteer, and hand them the white feather of cowardice. This actually occurred in numerous cases. Apparently the idea and the apprehension it engendered spread rapidly. One account is from the archives of the Imperial War Museum, quoted by Simkins in *Kitchener's Army*. Gunner H. Symonds, 182nd Brigade, Royal Field Artillery, gives us a flavour of what the white feather could mean to a young man:

> I was listening to a ginger-haired girl giving a recruiting speech at Hyde Park Corner on 24th July 1915. I was seventeen at the time, but eager to go. So when Ginger tucked a white feather into my buttonhole, I went off to the recruiting office.

The potency of this campaign was aided by the appearance on the streets of a poster which asked:

> Is your 'Best Boy' wearing khaki?
> If not don't you think he should be?
> If he does not think you and your country are worth fighting for –
> do you think he is worthy of you?

John Savage, in his book *Teenage*, argues that 'regardless of whether they were underage or already enlisted, every apparent shirker was a potential victim.' The white feather campaign remained in the public imagination long after the First World War. I recall my mother being in some fear that my father would receive a white feather since he was in a reserved occupation during the Second.

All the apparatus of imperialism was available in 1914 to support the spate of volunteering and to sustain the morale of the British Army and the British people through the war. In fact, it lingered on until its last gasp during the war against Argentina in the Falkland Islands. Imperialism, with its questionable attitudes to race and class, is alien to us now. The values by which our ancestors lived at the beginning of the twentieth century have been replaced with a new system, in which pacifism, multi-culturism, egalitarianism, feminism and greenism are fused into political correctness.

It is hard to enter the mind of a white male adolescent living in the first few years of the last century and understand what drove him to volunteer to fight in Kitchener's new armies, especially because the rules by which he lived and the ambitions he may have entertained have now become the subject of satire and ridicule. In fact, many of his values are seen as almost criminal. What motivated thousands of boys to volunteer to fight? Was it government propaganda? Were they duped or coerced? Was Kipling right when he wrote: 'If any question why we died ... tell them that our fathers lied'?

The Boer War was a first-class dress rehearsal for Armageddon. It attracted thousands of young lads to fight and die, yet lessons about recruiting and training which could have been learnt from it were ignored. The imperial myth continued to grip the public imagination, though the first fissures had appeared in the edifice of the Empire when the Boers showed the world how to beat the British Army. It is fair to suggest that there had been a long and powerful mobilisation of young minds for war before Kitchener called the British nation to arms in 1914.

In any attempt to write about the history of propaganda, the problem of changing language, and its effect on values, must be solved as early as possible. To us in the early twenty-first century, the word 'boy' tends to mean a male child, probably over-active, and not yet in puberty. We are now increasingly using the word 'youth' to classify the next stage of maturation, that of puberty and young manhood. From the mid-nineteenth century, almost to the mid-twentieth century, the word 'boy' was associated with manliness and pluck. 'Boys' were young males preparing to run the Empire.

The 1880 Education Act had raised literacy standards amongst school leavers and boys became the target audience for a particular genre of imperialist propaganda, in much the same way as the young today are the target audience for teen magazines, popular music, computer games and the repertoire of electronic media.

Between 1850 and 1914 child mortality had reduced and the population had doubled. Income had risen, but the cost of living had remained low. New methods of printing went hand in hand with the development of the railways and businesses specialising in the distribution and sale of printed matter. Improvements in the production of paper and the mechanisation of binding reduced the unit cost of producing books. All this allowed for massive print runs and the development of big publishing houses. Even more popular and influential were journals for boys, sometimes called the 'Penny Dreadfuls'.

By the start of the twentieth century, there were other developments which helped imperialism to become the dominant national ideology. Its symbols and stories pervaded newspapers, magazines, films, plays and music hall acts. It was conveyed in advertisements, prints, engravings, biscuit tin decorations, souvenir ephemera and cigarette cards. It began to pervade the schoolroom, the family bookcase, the sheet music in the parlour and the repertoire of bands playing in the public parks. It became a portmanteau concept embracing race, royalty, the armed forces, sportsmanship, chivalry and patriotism.[8]

The cumulative effect of the years of imperialist propaganda prepared the young male population to respond in droves to Kitchener's famous appeal for recruits in the early days of the war. As James Walvin wrote in a study of English childhood between 1800 and 1914: 'It is reasonable to assume that the adults who displayed such fierce nationalism in the early years of the century had learnt their jingoistic lines and acquired their sense of national superiority in their early formative years, when thumbing through their books, comics, magazines and yarns.'[9]

The inward thoughts, now sometimes called the mind-set, of the boys who readily offered themselves for sacrifice in the First World War, were profoundly influenced by the juvenile fiction of the day. The mind-set of those who allowed them to join the armed services may well have been affected also. Via the agency of popular stories for boys, a hero cult developed, as unlike as it could be from our modern idea of celebrity.

The pre-1914 hero, in his most popular fictional guise, was aged around fifteen or sixteen when he met with some family tragedy and was cast out into the harsh world. He became involved in one of the imperial wars, serving perhaps with Wolfe in Canada or Clive in India or Kitchener in the Sudan or Buller in South Africa. He acquitted himself brilliantly and performed a vital service, without which the great imperial enterprise would have failed. In doing so, he found his true identity and made enough money to return to England and settle down.

The superstar of boys' fiction writers was G.A. Henty. His publisher was to claim that he had sold 25 million copies of his novels, of which he published ninety or more, an achievement which bears comparison with the most prolific and popular writers of juvenile fiction today. Henty, who suffered from poor health as a child, was a mine owner's son. He went to Westminster School, where he was bullied, and took up boxing to defend himself. He gained a commission in the army commissariat during the Crimean War and later became a war correspondent. He witnessed most of the conflicts of the period, including the Austro-Italian war of 1861, the Abyssinian campaign of 1867, the Franco-Prussian war of 1871–2, the Siege of Khiva in the Russo-Turcoman war of 1873, the Ashanti war of 1873–4, the Carlist insurrection in Spain in 1874 and the Turco-Serbian war of 1876. He edited *Union Jack* between 1880 and 1883, contributed to *Boys' Own* magazine between 1888 and 1890 and founded *Camps and Quarters* in 1889.

Of the boy heroes of imperialist juvenile fiction, Henty's was the archetype; to understand him is to glimpse the ego ideal of a significant group of white male adolescents of the early twentieth century. Yorke Harbeton was a typical Henty hero. He was the sixteen-year-old son of the Rector of Waverfield in Somerset. He was educated at Rugby and was 'a typical public schoolboy – straight and clean limbed, free from all awkwardness ... a good specimen of the class by which Britain was built up – a class in point of energy, fearlessness, the spirit of adventure and readiness to face and overcome all difficulties unmatched in the world.'

Had Henty's openly class-laden material been read by public schoolboys alone, it would have been influential enough, but it was also read by working-class boys and was echoed in the boys' journals widely distributed and read by all classes. It engendered a dangerous sense of racial superiority, which entered the imagination of British boys.

A synopsis of one of Henty's stories, *With Buller in Natal*, serves as an adequate example. The story begins just before the hero, Chris, has to leave his home in the boom town of Johannesburg in the republic of Transvaal because the Boer War is about to begin. He is the son of a prominent British expatriate or *uitlander* who owns mines and other business interests.

> The lad was a fine specimen of the young Uitlander. A life passed largely in the open air, hard work and exercise, had broadened his shoulders and made him look at least a year older than he really was. He was a splendid rider and an excellent shot with his rifle, for his father had obtained a permit from the authorities for him to carry one, and he could bring down an antelope running at full speed as neatly as any of the young Boers. Four days a week he had spent in the mines, for his father intended him to follow in his footsteps, and he had worked by turns with the miners below and the engineers on the surface, so that he might in the course of a few years be thoroughly acquainted with the details of his profession.

Chris takes a hazardous train journey from the Transvaal into Natal and meets a score of fellow *uitlanders* of his age, who have also been sent out of danger by their parents. They elect him captain of their band, purchase horses from a farmer, form a troop of irregulars and attach themselves to a Captain Brookfield's fictional unit, called by Henty the 'Maritzburg Scouts'. Chris addresses his gang of young adventurers thus:

> We shall, of course, have bandoliers for our cartridges, and haversacks for our provisions and spare packets of ammunition. Not an hour must be lost in getting these things. I hear that Captain Brookfield, who came up to Johannesburg last year and stayed a fortnight with us, has raised a corps, which he has named the Maritzburg Scouts. I will call upon him this afternoon and tell him that there are one-and-twenty of us, all somewhere about my age, and that we mean fighting; and that as we all speak Dutch we think we can do more good by scouting about on our own account than by joining any regular corps; but that at the same time we should like, if there was anything like regular fighting, to place ourselves under the orders of an officer like himself. It is rather difficult to explain, you know, but I think he will understand what we mean. We should be, in fact, a section of his troop, acting generally on independent service, either scouting, or going in among the Boers and getting intelligence, trying to blow up bridges, and engaging looting parties – for we may be sure that the Boers will be scattering all over the country plundering.

The boys in the troop observe some of the major events of the war, such as the siege of Ladysmith and the Battle of Spion Kop. They have numerous adventures and, by good horsemanship, pluck and determination, acquit themselves as scouts and irregulars. Here, for example, is Chris reporting to Captain Brookfield about an independent action he and his band of boy soldiers had carried out to recapture cattle looted by Boer raiders:

> Yes, sir; we caught them as they were attacking the house at ten o'clock that night. They were too busy to notice us, and we killed eleven and wounded eighteen, and stampeded their ponies. They bolted on foot, but came back in hopes of surprising us two hours later, which I need hardly say they failed to do. Then they made off for the place where the herds they had captured were waiting for them. We drove their ponies in, as our own were too much done up to go on, and intercepted the Boers close to Inadi, and made them surrender. We took their guns, ammunition, and loot from them, and let them go. There were forty-nine of them altogether, and we did not see what we were to do with them. We could not have brought them here without the whole thing being made public, and we were certainly not disposed to escort them down to Maritzburg. They will have at least a hundred miles to tramp home. We recovered all the cattle, about two thousand head. We gave them to the farmers to find their proper owners, and thirty of the Boer horses that we captured. I dare say they will pick up some more of them; for as we were in a hurry, we only drove in as many as we wanted. We have no casualties. It could hardly be called a fight, it was a sudden surprise, and they did not stop to count us.

The war ends and Chris, having 'found himself' during his adventures, goes home to England and we assume that he will succeed in life. He is sixteen at the beginning of his adventure; the reader accepts that he should go to war as the leader of a troop of irregulars of the same age. He had left the kindly, protected world of childhood and ventured through the dark world of secret missions, narrow escapes, desperate fights and dramatic rescues. He overcame all odds to emerge into the light again as a tried and true English gentleman. Chris was, of course, an example of the white male ex-public school hero of popular 'Boys' Own' fiction. In the years just prior to the First World War, he, and his like, were to be incorporated into the inner personal narrative of thousands of male adolescents.

War was often used by Henty as the ordeal through which his hero must pass in order to reach manhood and become an English gentleman. The wars were always won by the British and, significantly for Henty's readers, the enemy was always portrayed as brutal, dirty, unscrupulous and racially inferior. Jeffrey Richards, sometime reader in History at the University of Lancaster, has highlighted a particularly telling phrase in the preface to *St George for England*, published by Henty in 1885, which charged the British male adolescent with a terrible burden:

> The courage of our forefathers has created the greatest Empire in the world around a small and itself insignificant island; if this Empire is ever lost, it will be by the cowardice of their descendants.

Henty believed it and so did many of his readers. It was a fatal ideal.

We should also remember that, for those who were not privileged to continue their education after the age of fourteen, the world of work commenced the day after leaving school. The number of unskilled jobs available for the fourteen- to seventeen-year-old boys was significant. Working-class boys were tea makers, hoddies, delivery boys, stable hands, brass polishers, boot boys and porters. This gave them a modicum of financial independence and they, too, became the target for new consumer products: clothing, entertainment, magazines and comics. It is, therefore, interesting to read the words of Fredrick Willis in his book *101 Jubilee Road*, published in 1948, describing the contents of the 'Halfpenny Dreadfuls', which had a wide circulation among working-class boys:

> Looking back nearly fifty years to what people read, the first periodicals that come to mind are the working boys' books, 'Pluck', 'Halfpenny Marvel' and 'Union Jack' … They all cost one halfpenny and had sixteen pages of closely-printed letterpress and five or six illustrations, the chef d'oeuvre being the illustration which was on the front cover and depicted the stirring incident from the story within. One complete story was presented each week, with a title such as 'Dead Man's Reef', 'Pirates of the Air', or 'The Great Thames Mystery'. It has been said of these three periodicals that recruiting sergeants felt that they did more 'to provide recruits for our Army and Navy and to keep up the

estimation of these services in the eyes of the people of this country than anything else'.

The comic *Magnet*, first issued in 1908, was said to have had an extraordinary influence on working-class boys. It serialised a story, written by Frank Richards, of a boy named Harry Wharton who attended a fictional public school called Greyfriars. Harry is sent to Greyfriars School by his uncle Colonel Wharton, described as a bronzed, grim-visaged old soldier, because he was becoming difficult. His adventures at school appealed to young male adolescents of all classes because of his undoubted pluckiness and his short temper. In the first issue of *Magnet*, the tone was set with descriptions of five fist fights. Greyfriars was depicted as typical of the public school of the day: a male-dominated, enclosed society. In it there were two cultures running alongside each other. One was the subculture, in which the secret life of Harry Wharton and his friends flourished according to Greyfriars rules – no hitting an opponent when he was down, no kicking, no weapons. The other was the official culture of prefects, school chapel and competitive sports. In his *Classic Slum*, Robert Roberts says:

> the standards of conduct observed by Harry Wharton and his friends at Greyfriars set the social norms to which schoolboys and some teenagers strove spasmodically to conform ... Through the Old School we learnt to admire guts, integrity, tradition; we derided the gluttons, the American and the French. [Greyfriars School] became for some of us our true Alma Mater, to whom we felt bound by a dreamlike loyalty ... the public school ethos, distorted into myth and sold amongst us in penny numbers, for good or ill, set ideals and standards. This, our own tutors, religious and secular, had singularly failed to do. In the final estimate it may well be that Frank Richards during the first quarter of the twentieth century had more influence on the mind and outlook of young working-class boys than any other single person, not excluding Baden-Powell.[10]

Pluck. A High Class Weekly Library of Adventures at Home and Abroad, On Land and Sea featured daring deeds in Afghanistan, South Africa, Egypt and India. There were stories about the Zulu, Matabele, Ashanti and Boer wars. *Union Jack*, which survived for forty years, was founded in

1880 by W.H.G. Kingston, a notable writer of boys' fiction. He died in 1880 and was succeeded as editor by G.A. Henty. Apart from writing for it himself, Henty commissioned stories from some of the great adventure story writers of the period, including Jules Verne, Arthur Conan Doyle and R.L. Stevenson. Another periodical, *Halfpenny Marvel*, contained stories of exploration, travel, the wonders of science and nature. In these and dozens of other titles, the world was presented as an adventure playground for British youth. Colonial wars were fought and won with the boy heroes playing a vital role.

There was also a flourishing market for biographies of real imperial heroes. Raleigh, Drake, Gordon, Cook, Livingstone, Lord Roberts, Rhodes and Kitchener found their way into *The Red Book of Heroes*, *Deeds that Made the Empire*, *British Solider Heroes*, *British Sailor Heroes*, *Brave Sons of Empire* and *Heroes of Britain in Peace and War*. Books such as these and the works of Henty, which contained the names of great men, were even used by teachers in school history lessons.

No discussion of the huge influence juvenile yarns had on adolescent minds leading up to the First World War is complete without a mention of *Boys' Own Paper* itself. It was the paradigm and the longest survivor of the breed, with the biggest circulation. In 1890 the total print run was estimated at 665,000. Since every copy sold was probably read by two or three other boys, it could have reached close to 1.4 million impressionable minds. It was founded by the Religious Tract Society in 1879 to counteract the effect of the 'Dreadfuls'. Strangely, one of its earliest and most important contributors lived a colourful life.

Dr Gordon Stables, who wrote a column for *Boys' Own Paper* called 'The Boy Himself', was a rather dangerous character who had been addicted to opium and chloral hydrate in his time. Later in life he became an alcoholic and was said to terrify the lads of Twyford, near Reading. He was often seen staggering out of his local pub, wearing a kilt and skean-dhu, leading a fierce dog and waving a cutlass, with which he threatened anyone in his path. His drinking bouts were legendary and he frequently suffered from delirium tremens. He was often drunk in charge of a strange vehicle he called the land yacht. This was a horse-drawn caravan, in which he travelled around the country with little regard for the rules of the road. That this admittedly colourful character should influence young lives at all seems strange, but he did.[11]

A new note of xenophobia crept into juvenile literature after the Boer War, with stories about the invasion of England by the French, the Germans or the Russians. The invasions were, of course, detected and beaten off by great imperial generals, naturally with the crucial intervention of a boy hero. The xenophobia was reflected in the theatre, with plays such as *Wake up England*, *Nation in Arms*, and *A Plea for the Navy*. Patriotic songs were a feature of pantomime. In 1911 the Drury Lane Theatre staged *Hop 'o my Thumb*, which contained a particularly paranoiac number. One verse makes the point:

> There are enemies around us who are jealous of our fame.
> We have a mighty Empire and they'd like to do the same.
> And they think the way to do it is to catch us as we nap.
> While they push our friends and neighbours from their places on
> the map.

> *Chorus:*
> And we mean to be top dog still.
> Bow-wow
> Yes we mean to be top dog still.[12]

Plays with a war theme began to dominate the London and provincial stage. In the two months of September and October 1914, twenty-four war plays or shows were licensed by the Lord Chamberlain. However, it was the cinema which led the charge to war. One of the few academics to make the point is Professor John Mackenzie, who stated unequivocally that 'war and alarms of war continued to be a cinematic obsession up to the First World War' and that 'such films contributed to the power of militarism of the period, and helped to prepare the way for the massive working-class recruitment to the army on the outbreak of the First World War.' The Volunteer Act of 1863 encouraged the formation of cadet corps. Thereafter, public schools formed corps, one of which, that of Reading School, is discussed in detail later. It is sufficient here to say that the movement spread throughout the classes; it expanded during the Boer War and afterwards was encouraged by the National Service League.[13]

The Boer War was not simply a military problem. It drew attention to that perennial of British complaints – anti-social behaviour and disaffected youth. As usual, a number of boy experts came to the surface, rather like the finger waggers of today who are diet experts or lifestyle gurus. The boy experts were sure that urban life was to blame for the failings of the British Army in the Boer War. Deference was disappearing. Poor posture and violent tendencies, they thought, were undermining the imperial edifice at its epicentre.

All this was certainly not lost on Robert Baden-Powell, the somewhat eccentric hero, who led the successful defence of the town of Mafeking, which had been besieged by the Boers. He used a great deal of initiative and imagination in defending the town and one of his innovations was the formation of the Mafeking Cadet Corps. This was a near military unit, made up of all the white boys aged between nine and eighteen living in the town. They carried messages, acted as lookouts and generally relieved the adult soldiers of tedious chores. Baden-Powell was eventually to say of them: '[The Mafeking Cadets] did not mind the bullets one bit. They were always ready to carry out orders, though it meant risking their lives every time.' This went some way to legitimise the recruitment of boys by the army.

Much effort and not a little paper have been expended in psycho-analysing Robert Baden-Powell. One of his biographers, Piers Brendon, has summed him up as 'a perennial singing school boy, a permanent whistling adolescent, a case of arrested development con brio.' Born in 1857, he was brought up by his mother; his father, an Oxford professor, died in 1860. He was educated at Charterhouse and joined the cavalry, serving in India and in the African colonial campaigns against the Ashanti and the Matabele. It was his instinctive empathy with boys which led to his most important contribution to the service of youth.

In 1903, fresh from his Mafeking success and from raising and commanding the quasi-military South African Constabulary, which had patrolled the wire fences and occupied the block houses in the guerrilla phase of the Boer War, Baden-Powell was invited to the annual drill inspection and review of the Boys' Brigade in Glasgow. Whilst he was there, William Alexander Smith, the Brigade founder, urged him to rewrite the army scouting manual, which he had published in 1899, to suit boys.

He took his Mafeking Cadets as the model for his now famous book *Scouting for Boys*, published in 1908. It was subtitled *A Handbook for Instruction in Good Citizenship* and was overtly imperialistic in tone.

The book consisted of twenty-six 'Camp Fire Yarns', each written to appeal to young male adolescents and, at the same time, to impart knowledge. The opening yarn was about the Mafeking Cadets. The emphasis was on adventurous but accessible outdoor life and practical survival. Many of the present-day survivalist handbooks are the direct descendents of *Scouting for Boys*. To make his points, he made use of what are now called role models, all of whom demonstrated selflessness.

Scouting for Boys became an international bestseller. In it Baden-Powell stated that every boy should learn how to shoot and obey orders so that they would be useful in time of war. He also emphasised the 'scouts of the nation', that is the pioneers, explorers and missionaries who had built the British Empire. Kipling's boy hero 'Kim' was held up as the ideal. Kim had been portrayed by Kipling as an effective intelligence agent, working to frustrate the perceived Russian threat to India.

The headings of his yarns are like a list of 'Boys' Own' adventures: 'Patriotism', 'How the Empire Grew', 'How the Empire Must be Held', 'The Song of Canada' and 'The Song of Australia'. Jon Savage argues that *Scouting for Boys* was saturated in the imperial ethos of muscular public school Christianity and cites these words of Baden-Powell as an example:

> Don't be disgraced like the young Romans who lost the Empire of their forefathers by being wishy-washy slackers without any go or patriotism in them. Play-up! Each man in his place and play the game![14]

Following the success of his books, he decided to form a series of local scout groups and the first troop was formed in Scotland by Captain R.E. Young in 1908. The Boy Scouts, as they became known, experienced a dramatic growth in numbers, with over 100,000 members by 1911.

After the outbreak of the First World War, the British government recognised the Boy Scouts. They did useful work in hospitals, at the Admiralty (where they acted as messengers), on the east coast and, in fact, anywhere they were wanted. On the east coast, a vast number of scouts helped the coastguards to watch for raiding German cruisers and it was a scout who first sighted an enemy cruiser off Hartlepool. Some Scout troops were sent to France to work in the base hospitals there.

The Boys' Brigade had been founded by William Alexander Smith in 1883. Its avowed purpose was to maintain young people's church attendance through the awkward teenage years. The boys wore a uniform consisting of a pillbox cap, belt and haversack. There was a heavy concentration on drill, for which dummy rifles were used. The Boys' Brigade expanded rapidly and by 1896 there were 264 companies in Scotland and 435 in England.

The Boys' Brigade and the Scouts were not intended as warmongering organisations when they were formed. Both turned down the opportunity to amalgamate with the Cadet Movement in 1910–11, despite losing money as a consequence. It is estimated that forty per cent of all males were in the Scouts, the Boys' Brigade or some other organisation between 1901 and 1920. These movements helped to mobilise young minds for the moment of recruitment in the Great War, a war which a significant majority of British people supported.

The issue of compulsory military service exercised British minds and divided opinion. Among its advocates was the National Service League, which had been formed in 1902. It has been called a militarist organisation and it was certainly led by a number of prominent people whose political views would today be called right wing. From 1905 to 1914 it was led by the imperial military hero, Field Marshal Lord Roberts of Kandahar VC. Under Roberts' charismatic and energetic leadership, the NSL became the most prominent of a number of patriotic organisations, such as the Navy League, the Legion of Frontiersmen, the First Aid Nursing Yeomanry, the Victoria League and the League of Empire.

The National Service League's main purpose was to advocate compulsory military service, based on a book by George R.F. Shea called *The Briton's First Duty: The Case for Conscription*, published in March 1903. In it Shea had warned that the nation was at risk because the Royal Navy alone was not sufficient for defence. He advocated a compulsory home defence army and, incidentally, that compulsory military service would counter the degeneration of youth and make better citizens, an argument often made to this day. Roberts had his own aims, which he did not make public. His intention was to promote conscription to raise a large army for a continental commitment against Germany. However, he and his fellow leaders were politically canny and realised that they would fail if they proposed conscription for foreign service. The NSL, therefore, advocated two months' training under canvass for all eighteen to twenty-two-year-old males, followed by brief annual training for three years, to form a citizens' army for home defence. Significantly, the League wished to see compulsory military training and drill in schools. To this end, Roberts sent a letter to all public schools, advocating national service.

In addition he transformed the NSL into a mass movement, which exploited every propaganda technique of the time. These included pamphlets, broadsheets, lantern slide shows, lectures, national campaigns and public meetings. There were also displays featuring the Territorials and the bands of the Church Lads' Brigade.[15]

From 1903 the League published *The Journal of the National Service League*, which became the *Nation at Arms* in 1906. It had an estimated circulation of over 47,000 and the *NSL Notes* reached 40,000 readers. By 1913 the League had a reputed membership of 96,526. It was producing and distributing films and gramophone records and had the support of the *Morning Post*, a conservative newspaper. In 1911–12 it held an average of 240 meetings a month and in the months leading up to the First World War it organised 2,500. However, it failed to achieve its immediate aim of conscription in 1914, as Kitchener opted for voluntary recruiting, but it raised the level of war fever and Germanophobia, thus indirectly boosting wartime volunteering.

In 1901 Lord Roberts had recruited Rudyard Kipling to write a poem to warn the British public of the need for compulsory military service. 'The Islanders' was the result. It created a furore and diminished Kipling's reputation as the great imperial poet. It was published in *The Times* by its editor, Bell, who was to become a supporter of the NSL. Some famous lines in 'The Islanders' discomforted the complacent gentlemen of Britain. It is a poem which can be read as an indictment of British failings in the Boer War and as a warning of German belligerence.

In 'The Islanders', Kipling wrote that the British preferred 'to train dogs and horses for sport instead of training men for soldiering.'[16] They had, he suggests, sent untrained and unfit city-bred boys to fight the Boer War on their behalf:

Sons of the sheltered city – unmade, unhandled, unmeet –
Ye pushed them raw to the battle as ye picked them raw from the street.

'The Islanders' also included one of the most celebrated and criticised lines Kipling was to write:

Then you returned to your trinkets; then ye contented your souls,
With the flannelled fools at the wicket or the muddied oafs at the goals.

The war with Germany, which Roberts and Kipling had predicted, came soon enough and Britain was unprepared. Unfit 'sons of the sheltered city' were sent to the front in their millions after the introduction of conscription in 1916. But it was the flannelled fools and muddied oafs who made the best soldiers.

3

ONE HELL OF A LESSON

But there are [sic], at any rate, a force which has helped us out of our present difficulties, which has stiffened the regiments, and given the country and all the world the proof that we have more soldiers in this country than they have ever given us credit for. And these are the boy soldiers, of whom it was said that they had no stamina, that they were recruited in such a manner that they would never be able to endure foreign service. Oh, those boys, how they fought in every part of South Africa!

George Joachim Goschen, First Lord of the Admiralty.
Speech to the 1st Middlesex Victoria and St George Rifles, 18 December 1899.

Winston Churchill was the war correspondent for the *Morning Post* during the Boer War. He managed to wangle a commission in the Imperial Light Horse, whilst he was in South Africa, so that he could also go medal hunting. In his book *My Early Life*, he wrote:

Let us learn our lessons. Never, never, never, believe any war will be smooth and easy, or that anyone who embarks on that strange voyage can measure the tides and hurricanes he will encounter. The Statesman who yields to war fever must realise that once the signal is given, he is no longer the master of policy but the slave to unforeseeable and uncontrollable events. Antiquated War Offices, weak, incompetent or arrogant Commanders, untrustworthy allies, hostile neutrals, malignant fortune, ugly surprises, awful miscalculations – all take their seat at the Council Board on the morrow of a declaration of war. Always remember, however sure you are that you can easily win, that there would not be a war if the other man did not think he had a chance.[1]

The Boer War had been brought to a painful halt in May 1903 by Kitchener's brutally effective anti-guerrilla tactics. As a result, he was promoted to full general, created viscount and given a bonus of £50,000. He had been directing the war since the departure of Lord Roberts in December 1901 and he was tired. Not everyone had agreed with his methods, though they were later adopted by British commanders against insurgents in Malaya. It is pertinent to ask what lessons Kitchener himself might have learnt from the Boer War, though, as always with bad administrators, there is little enough written evidence of his personal, rather than his official views.

His responsibility for the conditions which allowed the enlistment of boy soldiers during the First World War is sufficient reason to try and understand how Kitchener was influenced by his Boer War experiences. I argue that the Boer War reinforced Kitchener's conviction that the British Imperial Yeomanry was sent to South Africa insufficiently trained for the rigours of war and taught him never to send untrained men into battle again, if he could avoid it. I also argue that the rapid recruitment in 1901 of 17,000 volunteers for the second draft of the Imperial Yeomanry supported Kitchener's conviction that his call to arms in 1914 would be met with success. Significantly, and despite the obvious lesson of the Boer War, no attempt was made to plan for a rapid expansion of the army recruiting system in the event of a future emergency.

Kitchener's refusal in 1914 to allow the Territorial Force to recruit and train his new armies, or at least to form his 'first 100,000', still attracts criticism. Had it been given the task, it is very likely that it would have recruited boy soldiers. However, it might have been more responsive to calls to weed them out and send them home because of its strong local, and thus political, character. We will never know. The factors affecting

Kitchener's decision have been addressed by some outstanding scholars, including Peter Simkins in his brilliant book *Kitchener's Army, The Raising of the New Armies 1914–1916* and also by John Pollock in his thorough and readable biography *Kitchener*. Both of these scholars have made it clear that Kitchener scorned the Territorial Army and it is on this I would like to focus. I do so because Kitchener's direct and very personal influence on Asquith's cabinet and the War Office was, at first, enormous.

Peter Simkins and John Pollock both extensively quote reports of Kitchener's private views of the Territorial Force. They also refer to his disappointment with the Imperial Yeomanry volunteers in the Boer War. Simkins writes that 'claims have been made that Kitchener was far from enthusiastic about some of the Volunteer units which served under him in South Africa'[2] and Pollock asserts that Kitchener was 'influenced by a somewhat unhappy memory of the volunteer Imperial Yeomanry coming out to South Africa half-trained.'[3]

It is necessary to test these assertions – not least because there is evidence that the minimum age rule for recruits was flouted by the Imperial Yeomanry – but there is another reason: Kitchener was a strong advocate of voluntary recruiting, as we will see when we come to the issue of conscription. There were serious lessons to learn from the recruiting processes used to raise the second draft of Imperial Yeomanry. These have not often been examined.

A very brief summary of the Boer War follows. On 11 October 1899, Britain went to war with the Transvaal and the Orange Free State, the two Boer republics in South Africa. The war lasted until 31 May 1902 and cost the British government £210 million. According to Field Marshal Lord Carver, in his book *The Boer War*, 448,895 British soldiers served in the war with a total of 20,721 casualties, of which 7,582 were killed or died of wounds. Far and away the largest number of British fatalities, 13,139, succumbed to disease. On the Boer side, it is thought that a total of 87,365 men took up arms and that 7,000 were killed. In the later stages of the war, the British incarcerated Boer families, a total of somewhere between 18,000 and 20,000 people, in concentration camps – not to be confused with the death camps instituted by the Nazi regime in Germany but still not above criticism. The involvement of African natives is difficult to quantify but it is said that there were 10,000 armed Africans and up to 40,000 labourers and drivers on the British side. Estimates of native African casualties vary from 7,000 to 10,000.[4]

Much of the war was fought on the high *veldt*, a vast plateau intersected by a number of rivers and streams. This presented a series of obstacles to a large force of foot soldiers encumbered by a supply train. The area of operation was supplied with a network of railway lines, which was of great importance to the movement of men and stores. The *veldt*, with its strange assortment of hills, is a terrain where infantry, artillery and supplies move slowly and with difficulty, whereas it was ideal fighting ground for mounted infantry. The hills are known to the Boers as *kopjes*, a word which has been adopted by Liverpool football fans for part of their stadium.

The Boer force was made up of citizen soldiers between the ages of sixteen and sixty. They were organised into commandos, based on electoral wards or *wyks*. A commando could be anything from 300 to 3,000 strong, depending on the size of the *wyk*. On call-up, the commando gathered at the principal town and elected a commandant. Decisions were taken on a democratic basis by councils of war attended by all officers from the rank of corporal upwards. Although the citizen soldiers were amateurs, they were excellent horsemen and marksmen. They rode over the *veldt* on their ponies with speed and confidence, dismounting to fight with their superb rifles with disconcerting accuracy. They were probably the best mounted infantry in the world.

The average British soldier was not of sufficient general intelligence, fitness or adaptability to fight effectively in the new conditions of the war in South Africa. The figures quoted from Lord Carver's work show that a ratio of three British soldiers to each Boer soldier was needed to bring the war to a conclusion. The medical services on the British side were bad and there was little or no training in, or attention paid to, basic hygiene. Food, clothing and shelter were inadequate and water was drunk from rivers and streams, without due care and attention. The many deaths attributed to enteric fevers and dysentery are evidence enough of bad command and leadership.

The senior officers of the British Army were divided by faction. Not unlike Blairites and Brownites in the Labour Party of the late twentieth century, so called 'Rings' of opposing favourites had formed around the two most senior generals, Field Marshal Lord Roberts of Kandahar and Field Marshal Lord Wolseley, the commander-in-chief of the army. Wolseley's ring was in the ascendancy and Roberts was fobbed off with command in Ireland, from whence he intrigued with Lansdowne,

the Minister of War, to replace Wolseley. In the meantime, General
Sir Redvers Buller, a Wolseley man, was conducting the war against the
Boers in South Africa.

By the end of September 1899, Buller had already presided over a
number of defeats. During the years of imperial expansion, the British
had become accustomed to easy victories against weak opposition and
they did not take well to the news that the Boers had besieged British
troops in Ladysmith, Kimberley and Mafeking. Nor did they react
well to 'Black Week', in December 1899, when Gatacre was defeated
at Stormberg on the 10th, Methuen at Magersfontein on the 11th and
Buller at Colenso on the 15th. Field Marshal Lord Roberts, from his
backwater in Ireland, was stung by all this into sending a telegram to
Lansdowne, in which he proposed himself as Buller's replacement.
Lansdowne went to his prime minister with the telegram. In an astute
public relations coup, Lord Salisbury saw a way of relieving the public
sense of gloom caused by 'Black Week' – and of deflecting some of the
criticism – by appointing Lord Roberts VC, the sometime leader of
the famous Chitral Relief Column, to go out and save the army from
disaster. He cannily insisted that another public favourite, Major General
Lord Kitchener, the hero of Omdurman, should be sent along as well.

As a result, the diminutive sixty-seven-year-old Lord Roberts was
appointed commander-in-chief in South Africa above Buller. He took
Kitchener along as his chief of staff and the two of them arrived in
Cape Town on 10 January 1900. Buller took the news of his demotion
without apparent rancour and, during the weeks he remained in place
awaiting Roberts' arrival, he had plenty of opportunity to demonstrate
his incompetence as a general.[5]

Almost 45,000 men, a large part of the British Army, including many of
the militiamen who had volunteered for overseas service, were shipped
out to take part in the war, leaving Britain poorly defended. With this
massive army at his disposal, Roberts devised a plan which would use
the main railway lines from Cape Town right through the Boer republics
to Komati Poort on the borders between the Transvaal and Portuguese
East Africa. He would bring overwhelming force to bear on the Boer
capitals, while Buller remained in Natal to raise the siege of Ladysmith
and fight on as best he could.

Roberts' master plan was simple but flawed because it failed to
take into account the history and psychology of the Boers. Some of

their commanders, notably Prinsloo, capitulated but many, including Botha, de Wet, and Olivier, did not. Roberts' plan worked only as far as disciplined town–bred manpower could be deployed. The great columns of marching British soldiery and their wagon trains, raising clouds of dust to mark their whereabouts, plodding their disciplined way around the country with observation balloons floating above them, became an iconic image of the time. In contrast, the Boers had developed superb mounted infantry, which could move over great distances, amongst a sympathetic population, and appear and disappear with bewildering speed. Their prowess in this vital role was only partially matched on the British side by mounted infantry units raised from Australian, Canadian and South African volunteers, of whom there were not enough.

Buller realised this after the Battle of Colenso and sent the following telegram to Wolseley:

> Would it be possible to raise eight thousand irregulars in England? They should be equipped as mounted infantry, be able to shoot as well as possible and ride decently. I would amalgamate them with the Colonials.[6]

George Wyndham, Lansdowne's junior minister, embraced the idea and thus the Imperial Yeomanry was born, recruited partly from hunting farmers and horsemen. Some of the cost of raising it was found by private subscription, a good sum having been donated by Wernher-Beit, the Rand millionaire. It was amateurish, an admired quality at the time, but the calibre of recruit was better than that of the regular infantry. The British press and the people liked the idea of an elite corps and several thousand 'Gentlemen Rankers' enlisted, including stockbrokers, journalists and an MP. *The Times* of 4 January 1900 reported that among those who applied at the offices of the Middlesex Yeomanry there were many professional men holding good social positions and at least one well-known baronet. Altogether, around 35,000 men volunteered. Private individuals were also encouraged to raise volunteer units, among which was the Earl of Dunraven's 18th Battalion of the Imperial Yeomanry, known as the 'Sharpshooters'.

So, on 11 February 1900, Roberts launched his great flank attack on the main Boer centres of resistance with five divisions totalling about 40,000 men. He took Bloemfontein on 13 March, Johannesburg on 31 May and Pretoria on 5 June but allowed a large proportion of the Boer army to escape. Meanwhile, on 27 February, Buller raised the siege of Ladysmith. Later he broke through the Boer positions on the Drakensberg, taking Lydenburg on 6 September, and he sailed for England on 24 October. Roberts, prematurely proclaiming victory, annexed the Boer republics for the British Empire and then went home to achieve his most desired personal appointment. He replaced his great rival, Sir Garnet Wolseley, as commander-in-chief of the British Army. On 27 November 1900, Kitchener succeeded Roberts as commander in South Africa and presided over the guerrilla phase of the war against the Boers, whom the latter had failed to subdue.

The campaign was long and disgracefully bloody. The British proceeded to burn Boer farms, drive off their cattle and intern non-combatants. They built an immense network of blockhouses, joined by barbed wire, to divide rebel country into sections. They hunted the Boer commandos within the sections in what came to be referred to by the hunting, shooting and fishing fraternity as drives, forcing the Boers, like pheasants, up against stoppers formed by the wire fences and blockhouses. With their families incarcerated in camps and dying at an alarming rate, their homesteads burnt and their cattle driven off, the Boer commandos were eventually worn down. An armistice was signed and the war ended on 31 May 1902.[7]

The Imperial Yeomanry, when it was first raised, appeared to offer its potential recruits the veritable *Boys' Own* adventure, which had exerted its grip on the imagination of youthful British males for many years. The popular perception was that it would attract young men from among the yeoman farmers to fill its ranks. Yeoman farmers were just below gentlemen farmers in social rank and acreage farmed and it was hoped that some of the county gentry might join as officers. These yeoman farmers were believed to be intelligent, hardy, courageous and capable of independent action. It was thought that they already understood how to hunt, stalk game, ride and shoot. It was thus assumed that they would be a match for the Boer mounted infantry and, what is more, would need a minimum of training before being released on the enemy.

Recruitment was mainly on a county basis and in the hands of the local yeomanry regiments. By 1899 there were thirty-eight of these regiments in Britain, with a total establishment of 11,891 part-time soldiers and a permanent staff of 167 seconded from the regular army. They were, in fact, volunteer cavalry regiments raised by local landowners who, with their families, filled the commissioned ranks. Yeoman farmers, tenant farmers, huntsmen and horsemen filled the other ranks. The yeomen provided their own horses and were paid seven shillings a day during training. Recruits attended twelve drills and a musketry course for their initial training and subsequently six to eleven squadron drills each year. This was in addition to the eight days of annual training on the big estates owned by their officers, who enjoyed the benefit of military rank and the social gatherings in the big houses. For the officers there were the yeomanry exercises in the summer, pheasant shooting in season and fox hunting in the winter. This occupied the young bloods and kept them from going to the devil.[8]

Each of the county yeomanry regiments undertook to form a company of Imperial Yeomanry from among their number or from suitable civilian volunteers. These companies were brought together to form battalions of mounted infantry. By the end of January 1900, around 10,000 men had volunteered. A letter from a Reading parent, dated 21 January 1900, indicates that some young men were taken on with more enthusiasm than judgment:

> ... a very near relative of my own, a young man of 22, now writes to me that he has volunteered and been accepted for this [Imperial Yeomanry] corps. His upbringing has been essentially that of town and city, at school and college. Until his being put to the 'test' – which he was at Reading the other day – he never, I believe, fired a rifle in his life, although he has, no doubt (and this rarely), seen a sporting gun. As to riding, except on a very occasional holiday in the country, going along country lanes, he has had no experience, and grooming a horse, none. Three others, of similar class, have been accepted along with him ... there are plenty of rough riders and good marksman in the colonies, and this country, too, but young men like the above are not the sort required.

The young man's father may have been right. The life was, indeed, hard and the training period very short. For example, in January 1900, No. 6060 Trooper D.E.L. Holmes joined the 39th (Berkshire) Company, which formed part of the 5th Battalion, Imperial Yeomanry, and sailed for Cape Town on the *Norman* in February 1900. Extracts from his letters home appeared in *Old School Ties – Educating for Empire and War* by John Oakes and Martin Parsons. They were first published in the *Reading*

School Magazine in December 1903. Dennis Holmes was an old boy of Reading School and had joined with Lieutenant Giles Ayres, whose young relative and namesake we will come across later. The letters form a war diary which tells us a great deal about service in the Imperial Yeomanry, especially the hardships, as they rode and fought with Roberts during the 'Great Flank March'. Some extracts follow:

8th March 1900. Queenstown. We are still in camp; we arrived last Monday and expected to leave on Tuesday, but have had no orders yet, although there is a rumour that we leave on Monday for Naupoort [sic], and from there to Mafeking. We got our horses and had them out for drill the last two days. Mine is one that was captured from the Boers; they are all very small horses and fairly quiet. The weather is very hot in the daytime, and as there are 13 of us in a tent, we are generally warm at night. Today we are having an awful dust storm. The food we get is not bad; the meat is very tough, as it is only killed the night before. There is a canteen, where they sell tinned meat and lemonade. Pineapples we can get at 2d. and 3d. each. Captain Ricardo took most of us down to the baths in Queenstown yesterday afternoon. Our horses have been shod this afternoon. We have very little spare time, as we are obliged to take our horses 1 mile three times a day for water.

2nd April 1900. Near Kimberley. I have not tasted butter for a month and no bread for 10 days, only biscuits just like puppy cakes. We have been on the march again. And have just come back from a 10 days' march from Berkeley West; we came under Lord Methuen, and we got quite close to a lot of Boers, but the order came from Lord Roberts to go back to Kimberley by forced marches, and here we are just now, but we are likely to move any day to Boshof, and then to Bloemfontein. We had about six nights out in the rain with only one blanket over us, and a pool of water under us. We are now under canvass, and a good thing too, for the nights are very cold, and such heavy dews! Lord Methuen seems very pleased with us. I think we shall join Lord Roberts soon. About 12 Yeomanry here are now on the way to Pretoria as prisoners. I am glad I am not one of them. I am sitting on the ground with a bully beef tin to write on.

29th May 1900. Kroonstad. We got here after two weeks' march, and expect to start again tomorrow. The Boers were going to make a stand but we entered the place without firing a shot. Our Company is reduced to

70; all the others have dropped out from fever and dysentery, and some are on the way home.

4th June 1900. Lindley. We had some fighting; we drove the Boers back and took the town, but arrived two hours late to relieve the Yeomanry Regiment, which had surrendered. [This was the 13th Battalion Imperial Yeomanry in which a number of famous Irish aristocrats had enlisted. Their surrender created a great furore in the British press.] It was very hard luck, as we heard that they could hold out until Saturday afternoon, and we got here on Friday morning by a lot of forced marching. There are a lot of Boers still about; as I am writing I can see them about four miles away, and our outposts keep having a few shots. We only had two men slightly wounded. We were in two very hot corners. We expected to stay here for a day or two as our horses want rest; we have had three weeks on the move, a lot of forced marching, and left the Infantry and convoy a long way behind, and only Artillery and Yeomanry are in the fight; we had four horses shot, seven had a wash yesterday [sic], the first in twelve days; and last night my boots were off for the first time for a month; and then only because my feet are sore.

5th July 1900. Bethlehem. We are just going into Bethlehem. I do not know if we shall be opposed or not. We have had our camp shelled this morning, but the enemy have been in full retreat for two days, so I don't think they will make much of a stand, as we have General Clements on one side and I think General Hunter is not far away. We are with General Paget, and part of our Regiment is with Lord Methuen. The last two weeks we have been on short rations.

16th July 1900. Lindley. They tell us the war is nearly over, but we are busy as there are lots of Boers all round us here; they have sent in twice to ask us to surrender, but there is no danger of that, for we have a good position but not much food left; we have been on three-quarter rations for some time, and expect them daily to be cut down to half. We had a long ride last Monday, about 70 miles; we started about 7 p.m. and were in the saddle 10 out of 24, and two hours of the other on guard; we were mending telegraph posts, etc, which the Boers kept cutting. Last night the Boers shelled us for the first time; we got up at 3 a.m. and saddled and went back to bed.

AtVerliesfontein on 30 July 1900, Prinsloo surrendered 4,313 men, 3 guns, 2,800 cattle, 4,000 sheep, 5–6,000 horses and about 2 million rounds of ammunition in the Brandwater Basin. The surrender was said to be one of the great sights of the war. De Wet and a number of Boers managed to escape through a mountain pass that the British had left unguarded.

17th August 1900. Heilbron. I think it is the 17th, but I am not sure about it, and nobody seems to know. I have had no letters since April. I think we are stopping here for a few days. We are now attached to Generals Hunter and MacDonald; we were with the latter when Prinsloo surrendered. It took a whole week's fighting to catch that lot. We had a bit of a fight with Olivier when we came here. We have been three months on biscuits, and all the time have been on the move without tents. I have just had my hair cut for the first time for four months, a shave for the first time for three months, a wash for the first time for over a month, so feel quite 'smart'.

Shortly after writing the last letter, Dennis Holmes was taken ill with enteric fever and ordered back to hospital at Norval's Point, where he died on 5 September 1900.

Lord Roberts left Cape Town on 10 December 1900. He was beginning to doubt that the war was over, which is what he had believed six months previously. He must have realised that the Boer leaders, such as de Wet and Olivier, who had escaped from his clutches, had gone off to start the second phase of the war. His over-confident assertion that he had all but won cannot have helped his successor, nor did it help in recruiting replacements for the Imperial Yeomanry. The guerrilla phase of the war did not have patriotic appeal. It was dirty work and Kitchener was left to get on with it with diminishing support from the government at home. His strategy of using military columns 2–3,000 strong, centrally directed by himself and supported by ever-increasing farm destruction, used more soldiers than the newly elected Conservative government was happy to finance. His problem was exacerbated because many of the reserve and volunteer forces raised in Britain, such as some members of the Imperial Yeomanry, were going home, having completed the period for which they had volunteered.

In the new year of 1901, the government agreed to provide Kitchener with some 30,000 reinforcements. In January this notice appeared in *The Times* and other newspapers:

IMPERIAL YEOMANRY ADDITIONAL DRAFTS

The Field Marshall Commander-in-Chief Earl Roberts invites the attention of officers commanding Yeomanry brigades and regiments to the Royal Warrant and Army Order regarding the reinforcement of the Imperial Yeomanry.

In doing so he desires to express a hope that the call to arms for more men will meet with the same ready response which attended the original organisation of this fine force, and everything possible may be done to facilitate recruiting. He is glad to bear testimony to the excellent service and gallant behaviour of the Imperial Yeomanry in the field, and hopes to find their comrades at home will come forward to make good casualties and to relieve some now in the ranks who have rendered such faithful service to their country at a period of emergency.

The Special Army Order called for an additional 5,000 recruits. The qualifications for service included an age of between twenty and thirty-five, a height of no less than 5ft 3in, a chest measurement of at least 34in and a minimum weight of 115 lbs. The recruits were to prove to officers commanding yeomanry regiments that they were good riders and marksmen, according to yeomanry standards. Candidates were to be physically fit for service but the following addendum to this clause had serious repercussions later:

In carrying out the medical examination of candidates it should be borne in mind that it is unnecessary that they should fulfil the conditions of fitness required of a recruit enlisting for the full term of service in the Regular Army. It is sufficient that the candidate should be free from organic disease or other defects likely to prevent him from doing his work during the duration of the present war.

There was, at first, an encouraging response. One glorious example, which should have been a lesson for those engaged in recruiting some thirteen years later, was that of the famous Sharpshooters. The following report appeared in *The Times*:

… animated scenes last night at 13a Cockspur Street, where the offices of the Sharpshooter Corps of the Imperial Yeomanry are situated. Though affiliated to the main body, the Sharpshooters have their own organisation and are quite ready to begin the work of recruiting, though it must be confessed that a room reached by three narrow flights of stairs was hardly an ideal recruiting place. Up these stairs, nevertheless, the candidates began to struggle at 9 o'clock in the morning, and by 7 o'clock that night 140 applications had been filled in, while 40 men had been medically examined, of whom 30 were certified as medically fit. In addition to this there were at least 50 who were not thought at all suitable, and were rejected at once. So great was the rush that at one time the supply of forms was exhausted, and a pause followed until more were obtained. But the great excitement of the day was between 2 and 4, when the medical examination of the candidates took place. So great was the rush that men almost fought with one another in their eagerness to get to the doctor, and inasmuch as most of those who were awaiting their chance had unbuttoned their garments, and otherwise prepared themselves for medical examination so as to economise time, the scene was not without an element of the grotesque.

But recruiting soon stalled. Word of enteric fever, dysentery and other ills, which had devastated the Imperial Yeomanry in South Africa, must have leaked out. News of the change in the nature of the war would certainly have circulated among potential recruits. There is plenty of evidence that the pool of good quality recruits had been thoroughly drained in the first draft. What is more, the drafts were shipped out inadequately trained. Someone using the *nom de plume* 'Yeoman' wrote in *The Times* on 27 August 1901:

It is obvious from Lord Kitchener's report [emphasis added] that the second contingent of Yeomanry, whatever it has since become, was not in the first instance to be compared with the force which went out in the earlier part of 1900, and which has earned so splendid a reputation ... The original body of Imperial Yeomanry was ... mobilised at the headquarters of the county Yeomanry regiments, the officers of which were on duty during the whole period of mobilisation purchasing horses and saddlery, drilling men and horses, and doing their utmost to turn out a body of men who would do credit to their regiment. Equipment and clothing was purchased and fitted, and would-be recruits were put through riding and shooting tests. In the case of the men with whom I was associated these duties were carried out for two months ... solely by the officers of the county regiments. The requisite tests for qualification were scrupulously carried out throughout the force ...

The officers of the first contingent were, as a rule ... taken from the county Yeomanry regiments, and were country gentlemen possessing all the qualifications which Lord Chesham enumerated as essential. Now compare this with the course pursued with the second contingent. The officers were, as a rule, subalterns of Yeomanry who had joined since 1900 and infantry Volunteer officers possessing no knowledge of mounted or stable duties. No one of the rank above subaltern was accepted. The men were recruited haphazard, and sent off as soon as possible to Aldershot without any test of shooting and horsemanship. There they were assembled, and drafted off to the Cape as opportunity afforded. No doubt the officer in charge of the Aldershot depot did all that was possible for man to accomplish; but there can be but one opinion as to the respective merits of the two systems; and it is hoped that should a similar force ever have to be mobilised again, the War Offices will lay to heart the lesson we have learned ...

The Royal Commission on the War in South Africa, reporting in August 1903, made a number of comments about the second draft of Imperial Yeomanry. They were cautious but it is clear that few of the recruits were able to ride and to look after a horse. There was no time to train the men on their arrival in South Africa, as they had to take to the field almost immediately. Of their officers, many were unable to ride and, of the 400 who went out to South Africa, 103 had to be sent home for one reason or another. It was a farce which made Kitchener angry. Another, more disturbing picture emerged. Letters began to appear in the press, such as this one from a London clergyman, printed in *The Times* on 9 April 1901:

... seventy or 80 of our parishioners have been at the front and many have died for their country, showing, I doubt not, courage and discipline worthy of the best traditions of the Army. But it is a very different thing to take lads of 17 and call them at least 20, to transport them from the desk to the front, call them Imperial Yeomanry and pay them about four times the pay of the trained Regular, and put them on horses and expect them to follow successfully after Boers who can ride and know the country.

They can hardly have learnt horsemanship on board the transport, and if they are mounted on such horses as the war demands their horse must for long present more terrors than the enemy.

A letter from Sister Katherine Nisbet of the Imperial Yeomanry Hospital, Pretoria, quoted by Lord Carver, supports the London clergyman's view:

> ... these new Yeomen are for the most part under sized, pale and seedy looking youths of 18 & 19 yrs. old. This hospital is already full of them & they come up from Elandsfontein in almost daily batches of 20 or 30. Many are being returned home as unfit & they say quite openly, almost braggingly, that they came out for the trip for their health. Many have heart disease, some pthisis, some no teeth, others surgically unfit & won't be operated on for fear they become fit. Really it is a scandal and ought to make a bother at home ... there is one brilliant exception and that is the Sharpshooters.[9]

The Boer War focused an unwelcome and searching spotlight firmly on the army. It was not only the Imperial Yeomanry that had taken liberties with the lower age limit for recruitment. People had now become suspicious of the regular army. A letter about army pay and messing allowances in *The Times* of 24 April 1901 states in part:

> as no attempt is made to ascertain the real age [of recruits], and as children of 14, 15 and 16 are enlisted, it is impossible to arrive at a just average. That average is probably well under 18 on enlistment. Without full data it is, of course, impossible to give exact figures; but the enormous loss arising from the enlistment of boys is evident ... At a moderate estimate it appears that there can hardly be in the ranks less than 60,000 lads ... How many soldiers under 20 have been sent to the front we can never know.

There is one further sad tale. In 1903 drafts were still being sent to South Africa to deter any possibility of resurgent Boer unrest. *The Times* of 17 March 1903 included this report from its special correspondent in Bloemfontein:

> British officers are complaining bitterly of the class of recruits now arriving. In one draft the average age of the soldiers was 18, and there

were a few who were far younger, mere boys of 14, although they were enlisted as being the proper age. The officers say that it is impossible to train these growing lads as they are unable to bear the strain of hard work in a new climate. The Dutch openly scoff at the youthful appearance of the recruits, while other soldiers christen their new boy comrades after the Secretary of War whose name has become a generic term for them.

The secretary of state for war at the time was St John Brodrick. Old soldiers are good at finding just the right word for those things which make their life difficult. 'Brodricks' fits into the cannon of military slang comfortably and would have tripped off the tongue of a seasoned sergeant major with ease and not a little satisfaction.

St John Brodrick had taken over as secretary of state for war from Lansdowne in 1901 and had put forward proposals for the reorganisation of the army. He argued that the Boer War had shown that organisation should be improved and that Britain should be able to send three army corps abroad as well as maintaining a properly organised force at home for defence. There was a requirement for more artillery and mounted troops, a reformed medical service, better transport, better trained officers, less barrack square drill, more musketry, scouting and individuality. Brodrick's proposals raised hopes that grown men could be attracted to the regular army and thus diminish its reliance on an inordinate number of immature boys, of whom a large percentage never became soldiers. However, there must have been a very large number of 'Brodricks' in the army.

The Royal Commission on the War in South Africa opened its proceedings under the chairmanship of the Earl of Elgin on 11 October 1902. It examined evidence from thousands of witnesses, including Lords Roberts and Wolseley as well as Kitchener himself. Its conclusions were published in January 1903 and it would be ridiculous to imagine that they passed Kitchener by. He would have been deeply interested in the remarks about his own performance, if nothing else. It gave some thought to the Imperial Yeomanry.

After acknowledging that many of the second draft of recruits were unable to ride and shoot and that their officers were in much the same boat, it stated that experience turned them into better than average soldiers and that:

the contrast between the First and Second contingents of the Imperial Yeomanry is interesting as showing, firstly, that in a time of national emergency and emotion a picked force of the best fighting material can be obtained, and, secondly, that, when the crisis has passed and the emotion has declined, it is possible, especially if trade is bad and there is a chance of doing better in a new country, to obtain for 5s a day, a class of recruits, looked at as raw material, of better average quality than that obtained at the ordinary rate of pay in the Army.

The Commission went on to suggest:

it would have been wise to have raised and trained drafts to reinforce the Imperial Yeomanry and … the necessity avoided of sending out 17,000 untrained and unorganized men to receive their education in the face of the enemy in some ways skilful and by this time veterans, though not very numerous.

In early August 1914, Colonel Repington, the military correspondent of *The Times*, met Kitchener and subsequently reported the detail of the conversation:

Lord Kitchener's new army, of which the skeleton of the infantry organisation has already appeared, is to be an army raised for the war and to be disbanded at the peace. It is enlisted for three years or the time of the war, and whenever the war ends the army will disappear. It is not practical in ordinary times to maintain an army larger than we already possess, and Lord Kitchener is well aware of the fact. But under stress of patriotic feeling recruiting is always brisk, and on this occasion when public spirit is high, and so many hands are thrown out of work by the war, there has been a rush to join, and in a week or a fortnight the first 100,000 will be made up.

Kitchener's reported views bear a remarkable similarity to those expressed by the Elgin committee.

The Boer War, if it achieved nothing else, made a thorough reorganisation of the British Army inevitable, because of the findings of the various boards of inquiry and commissions set up to learn from it. Without these changes, it would have been impossible to fight the First

World War. It is the plight of boy soldiers in this war which is the focus of our interest. It is not the lessons learnt by Haig, French, Hamilton and others, who went on to high command in the First World War, but it is the sergeants in the recruiting offices, who watched as our boys filled in their attestation forms and lied about their age, that interest us. We need to ask why the 'Dug Outs', the veterans of the Boer War and the Sudan who trained recruits at Aldershot or the Curragh, did not weed them out and send them home. The answer may be simple – but one more Boer War story will make the point.

The Liberal MP John Markham had been crusading on behalf of some soldiers whom he thought had been treated harshly by courts martial. One of them was Henry Mellon. Markham had been asking about him in Parliament for some time, without success. He was angry enough to write this letter to the editor of *The Times* which was published in the newspaper on 17 September 1901:

> Before the prorogation of Parliament I directed attention to the case of a youth named Henry Mellon, in the Black Watch Highlanders, who had enlisted when under 16 and is now only 17 ½ years of age, was in 13 engagements in South Africa, and after being kept almost continuous marching, was found asleep from physical exhaustion when on duty and sentenced to two years' imprisonment, several months of which he had undergone in the prison in Wakefield. I pointed out that the boy had two well conducted brothers in the Army and another in the Navy, and his parents were in distress on account of what they considered his harsh treatment. Lord Stanley at once intimated that the youth would be released; but on enquiring some time after why he had not been released it was announced that the release would only take place on the day when he would be embarked for South Africa. An appeal was made to allow him a fortnight's furlough to see his parents before being shipped off, but this was refused; and at this moment they do not know whether he is still in prison or has been sent back to South Africa.

Henry Mellon was aged seventeen years and six months in September 1901. If he survived the war and continued to serve in the Black Watch, he would have been some 30 years old in 1914 when Kitchener called for volunteers. Let us hope that he had lived down the experience of prison and gained some rank and status in the army. Perhaps not, but his like could well have found comfortable billets as recruiting sergeants in London or drill instructors at Aldershot. To the average recruiting sergeant, a sometime 'Brodrick' in South Africa perhaps, underage recruits were nothing unusual. He could easily have suggested to a sheepish boy, who blurted out that his age was seventeen and a half, that he might go for a walk and that when he got back his age would be nineteen.

Other lessons were learnt, which were important for our boy soldiers. The rejection on medical grounds of forty per cent of volunteers for the Boer War led to some vital changes in children's health services and education. The Committee on Physical Deterioration was established in 1904, followed by the provision of school meals in 1906, medical inspection in 1907 and grants for medical treatment in 1912. It also led to the development of shooting clubs in schools, justified on the grounds that Boer children were taught to shoot when they were young.

Kitchener and David Lloyd George, the First World War prime minister, were uneasy bedfellows during the latter's tenure as secretary of state for war. The antagonism may have first arisen during the Boer War, which was opposed by Lloyd George and his friends in the radical wing of the Liberal Party. Lloyd George toured the main British cities, making great use of his public speaking talents to condemn the Boer War. Some of his speeches were inflammatory and aroused sufficient protest to require police protection. It is easy to imagine Kitchener, who was getting on with the dirty business of fighting a war on behalf of the politicians, fuming and fretting at being undermined by radicals at home. Some of Lloyd George's political friends of the time commenced to ask questions in Parliament to embarrass the government – but not to question the conduct of the Boer War outright. One of them was Arthur Markham, who used the ploy of questioning soldiers' pay and underage recruiting; the same ploy he was to use during the First World War to embarrass Kitchener.

Early in the war the Boers laid siege to elements of the British Army in Ladysmith, Kimberley and Mafeking. In doing so the Boers dissipated much of their strength. They might have been better to have used all of their forces to make a pre-emptive sweep into the Cape Colony and Natal, raising the Afrikaner inhabitants as they went and capturing the ports of Cape Town and Durban. Had they done so before the British could land massive reinforcements at Cape Town, they might have won the war.

4

RECRUITING FEVER

Smiling they wrote his lie; aged nineteen years.
Germans he scarcely thought of; all their guilt,
And Austria's, did not move him. And no fears
Of Fear came yet. He thought of jewelled hilts
Of daggers in plaid socks; of smart salutes;
And care of arms; and leave; and pay arrears;
Esprit de corps· and hints for young recruits.
And soon he was drafted out with drums and cheers.

From 'Disabled' by Wilfred Owen.

The prospects facing the British people in July 1914 were not good. War on the continent was a distinct possibility. Ireland was in turmoil. The Liberal government, led by Asquith who was sometimes the worse for drink, was not doing well. There had been some civil unease in England. Asquith had taken the War Office into his own hands as a consequence of the British Army's Irish troubles, known as the 'Curragh Incident'. It is clear that he was unaware of the magnitude of the crisis his government faced, culpably so some would say. However, Viscount

Herbert Horatio Kitchener, the British Agent in Egypt, was in England on leave.

On Bank Holiday Monday, 3 August 1914, Kitchener's leave was over and he was on his way back to Cairo. He was standing on the deck of the cross-channel ferry in Dover harbour, fretting at some delay or other, when he received a note from Prime Minster Asquith asking him to break his journey and return to London.

Ostensibly Asquith wanted to consult him about the imminent violation of Belgian neutrality by the German Army but he also had other motives. Kitchener's prestige among the British people was enormous. Perhaps the best, but inaccurate, comparison is with Winston Churchill's standing after his famous radio broadcasts in the Second World War. Kitchener was an asset Asquith could exploit politically, if he could find a way of doing so.

On 4 August 1914 the Germans did invade Belgium, despite an ultimatum from the British. War was declared and the British Expeditionary Force and the Territorial Force were mobilised. Kitchener and Asquith held a fateful meeting that evening between 7 and 8 p.m. There are no notes of what transpired but it seems that Kitchener may have threatened to return to Cairo, unless Asquith made him secretary of state for war.

Asquith, whose cabinet was divided over the matter, dithered for a few hours but on 5 August Kitchener got the job he wanted and the government abandoned civilian control over grand strategy at a crucial time. There was an alternative candidate, whose appointment might well have changed history. He was Lord Haldane, the Scottish lawyer and sometime Liberal MP. He had been secretary of state for war from 1905 to 1912 and had carried through some vital reforms of the army following the Boer War. He had been educated in Germany and was wrongly accused of German sympathies. Had he been appointed, there would have been a press furore but the cabinet would have retained control of grand strategy. Haldane was to leave the Liberal Party for the Labour Party after the war.

The impact of Kitchener's appointment on the British people was enormous and was summed up in a paragraph written by F.S. Oliver in his book *Ordeal of Battle*:

No appointment could have produced a better effect upon the hearts of the British people and upon those of their Allies. The nation felt – if we may use a homely image in this connection – that Lord Kitchener was holding its hand confidently and reassuringly in one of his, while with the other he had the whole race of politicians firmly by the scruff, and would see to it that there was no nonsense or trouble from that quarter.[1]

Kitchener's life story is well known. A brief outline will serve as a reminder. He was a product of the Royal Military Academy, Woolwich, where he trained as a Royal Engineer. While still a cadet he witnessed the Franco-Prussian War, an experience which is said to have influenced him when making decisions in 1914. He proved himself with a masterly survey of Cyprus and was later deeply involved in the events leading up to and following the death in Khartoum of General Gordon. As a result, he was made commander-in-chief (*sirdar*) of the Egyptian Army in 1890.

He spent the following years in Egypt training men and husbanding stores to avenge the death of Gordon and rescue the Sudan from the rule of the fanatical khalifa and his dervishes. In 1898, after he was fully prepared, he moved up the Nile and won the Battle of Omdurman. This is too often overlooked when reviewing Kitchener's preparation for the First World War. The Battle of Omdurman was a relatively easy victory, once Kitchener's army had been transported, by rail and water, from its bases in Egypt to its confrontation with the dervish army in the Sudan. Kitchener had a railway built through miles of desert to transport men and supplies. It was a superb feat of logistics and engineering, accomplished through patience and determination. The preparation was repeated on a larger scale when Britain raised, trained, supplied and delivered a mass army to fight on the Western Front. As a reward for his Sudan campaign and his deft dealings at Fashoda with a French challenge to British claims on the Sudan, Kitchener was created a baron and appointed governor general of the Sudan.

During the Boer War, Kitchener was chief of staff to Lord Roberts. He succeeded Roberts in 1900 and waged an unpopular guerrilla war against stubborn Boer commandos. His reputation for unorthodox leadership and lack of attention to detail earned him the nickname 'Kitchener of Chaos'. He was chronically unable to delegate, a trait which was to undermine him during the First World War.

He was awarded the Order of Merit and in 1902 was made commander-in-chief in India. During his tenure of this post, he became famous for his quarrel with Viscount Curzon, the viceroy, about the command of the Indian Army. In 1911, by now a field marshal, he returned to Egypt as Britain's de facto ruler. He was still in that post when Asquith appointed him secretary of state for war. He had been overseas for so long that he had scant knowledge of, or patience with, British ways of working.

Kitchener's immense prestige in Britain was his greatest asset but he was not universally popular. Lord Curzon wrote to Lansdowne after Kitchener's untimely death by drowning in June 1916, when HMS *Hampshire*, taking him to Russia, was sunk by a German mine.

> … the papers and the public have got the wrong end of the stick about K [Kitchener]. 'Genius for organisation', 'wonderful foresight' – alas, as we know only too well, the very things he has not got. His death came in a most fortunate hour for his reputation. For he will not always be a national hero.[2]

On the afternoon of 5 August 1914, a meeting of the ad hoc council of war took place in Downing Street. In attendance were Asquith, the prime minister; Sir Edward Grey, the foreign secretary; Winston Churchill, the first lord of the Admiralty; Haldane; Field Marshal Lord Roberts of Kandahar, sometime commander-in-chief of the army; Sir John French, the commander-in-chief of the British Expeditionary Force; and a number of senior army officers, including Sir Douglas Haig.

The meeting had been called to make decisions about the British Expeditionary Force and its disposition in France. There was another reason, however, why this meeting was crucial. With absolute conviction, Kitchener announced that the war would last for three years. This astonished the others, with the possible exception of Haig, who were of the opinion that it would be over by Christmas. They believed that the large French Army, assisted by the BEF, would overcome the Germans quickly. It is likely that the British public was also of this opinion and was to remain so for some time. This public optimism may have dissuaded a number of parents from forbidding their underage sons to volunteer. To them and their sons it may have looked like another of those brief *Boys' Own* adventures, where young British heroes save the day and come home covered in glory.

Kitchener further astonished the meeting by stating that he would have to raise an army of a million men, including 100,000 immediately, in order to defeat the Germans. Despite some reservations, the rest agreed to go along with his plan, which amounted to nothing short of turning Britain from a maritime power into a temporary military nation. They left it to him and he was, as his biographer John Pollock says:

> uninhibited by his lack of close knowledge of British industries and politics, caused by long years of duty abroad. He met the country's urgent need unbothered by doubts as he set about raising the first hundred thousand.[3]

So, once more in her history, Britain was forced to do what she had hitherto refused to contemplate and raise an army. This time her task was gigantic and unprecedented. She could not, like the Germans, draw on a core of trained officers and NCOs. The New Army had to be raised and trained from scratch. This flew in the face of military dictum, which stated that armies could be expanded to a limited extent but not improvised anew.

The undertaking was made more than usually difficult because, for ancient and deep-seated reasons, there was no proper register of men eligible for military service. What is more, both Kitchener and the Liberal government refused to countenance conscription; Kitchener because he wanted a volunteer army for motivational reasons and the government because conscription was opposed by powerful forces on the left and right of the political spectrum. Instead there was to be a call for volunteers; at first the 'hundred thousand' and then as many as would be needed or could be recruited. Kitchener's personal appeal went out on 7 August 1914 and was later immortalised by the famous poster in which his face appeared with the legend 'Your Country Needs You'. Kitchener's New Army was born.

When searching for the one person most responsible for the recruitment of so many underage soldiers in the Great War, it is too easy to single out Lord Kitchener of Khartoum, who alone made the decision not to use the Territorial Force to recruit and train his new armies. It had been envisaged by those who formed the Territorial Force that its County Associations would oversee any future expansion of the army. In hindsight this sounds plausible but it overlooks Kitchener's insistence that his new armies should be thoroughly trained before they were sent to the front. He wanted the training to be under his direct control and would brook no interference from the local Territorial Associations. It is, however, rightly argued that his decision to use the regular army recruiting organisation caused it to be immediately overcome by a flood of eager volunteers. It was accustomed to dealing with 30,000 recruits a year but found itself swamped by that many in a week. The chaos in the recruiting offices resulting from this early flood of recruits added to the reasons why underage recruits were able to enlist.

On 10 August 1914 *The Times* carried three significant reports. In one it described the German attack on the Liège Forts in Belgium, probably one of the key moments in the war. The second was a report about the mobilisation of the British Expeditionary Force which was gathering at Aldershot, and the third concerned the response to Kitchener's famous appeal for volunteers. It is worth quoting in part:

> The influx of recruits continues. The number actually enrolled at the various recruiting offices in London in the last 24 hours was about 1,100 men. At the central recruiting offices at Great Scotland Yard throughout Saturday there was a large queue of men waiting to enlist. Although the large number of men mentioned in the War Office statement was enrolled, there were left at the end of the day 500 or 600 men who could not be dealt with. New recruiting offices are being opened ...

From this we can deduce that the rush of volunteers overwhelmed the recruiting officers and their staff. If this were an isolated incident related to the events in Belgium, it would have been interesting enough but it was not. The shambles at the recruiting offices had commenced earlier. Peter Simkins writes:

> On Saturday 1 August only eight men had been attested at the principal recruiting office of Great Scotland Yard and the following days were a Sunday and a bank holiday, yet when the recruiting officer arrived on the morning of the 4th August he was confronted with a mass of volunteers waiting to enlist. Even with the help of a score of policemen it took him twenty minutes to force his way inside ...

On 6 August there were 700 men left outside the recruiting offices when they closed at 4.30 p.m.[4]

On 11 August a marquee had been erected on Horse Guards Parade to alleviate the pressure on the offices at Great Scotland Yard and 100 recruits were being attested per hour. The average peacetime rate of attestation was 100 a day for the whole of Britain. The picture is clear. The system was overwhelmed. Lord Esher wrote in his journal on 12 September that 'military arrangements are thrown into confusion owing to our Secretary of State's inexperience of our organisation at home. If he persists in raising this new army, I am afraid he will destroy the morale of the Territorial Force.'[5] However, a report in *The Times* on 12 August 1914 indicates that not every eligible young man was rushing to the recruiting offices:

> there are a large number of footmen, valets, butlers, gardeners, grooms and gamekeepers, whose services are more or less superfluous, and can either be dispensed with or replaced by women without seriously hurting or incommoding anyone ... there are also thousands of adult caddies, green keepers, and other ministers of sport whose enlistment in the service of the King would benefit their country, themselves and even those who ordinarily employ them.

We begin to see another reason why underage recruits were encouraged to sign up: a large number of eligible men were not volunteering. As the flow of eager volunteers began to slow and demand for recruits increased, pressure to fill quotas became intense. Adolescents were, as we will see, easy targets.

The volunteer recruiting peak occurred on 3 September when 33,204 men were attested. On 4 September 1914 *The Times* reported:

> the Second Battalion of the London Scottish was completed yesterday, the Lord Mayor of London is raising a battalion of businessmen 1,500 strong, and defraying all the expenses: The total number of recruits accepted at Bristol now exceeds 3,000, a number that would have been doubled but for the strict medical tests: In Manchester 20,000 have been enlisted ... our young men are answering the call and presenting themselves faster than the recruiting stations can deal with them. That at least is the case in London, and returns for the whole country are at the rate of 30,000 a day ... this represents a great increase in the volume of the candidates ... we believe the main reason to be a fuller and more general realisation

of the need … our people are always slow to grasp new ideas or a new situation which does not accord with their regular habits, so that the conviction that the time has come for defending all that we hold dear, by force of arms and all the manhood we possess, has been slow in permeating the intelligence of the people. When it does they respond with all the old spirit. What has brought the truth home to many this week is neither taunts nor threats, but the return of the wounded from the war, which is often the first that is known of their heroism.

The returns show that between 4 August and 12 September 478,893 men had joined the army. New recruiting offices had been opened quickly to deal with the wave of volunteers. Many of these were in schools closed for the summer holiday. For example, on 10 August it was reported that offices had opened at Francis Street, Woolwich; 22 Grove Crescent Road, Stretford East; Everington Street Council School, Edgware Road, Marylebone; Grafton Road Council School; and Seven Sisters' Hall, Peckham Road. However, it was ludicrously easy for young men to lie about their age. At the rate at which men were attested, the policy of 'if they are big enough, they are old enough' can have been the only criterion. No birth certificate or other proof of age was required. The recruit merely had to sign an attestation form, on which he could lie about his age and his name. Many thousands did both.

It is not surprising that recruiting sergeants bent the rules. At first they were paid five shillings for each man joining the Foot Guards, the Royal Artillery, the Royal Engineers or the Mechanical Transport Section of the Army Service Corps. They received two shillings and six pence for recruits who joined cavalry and infantry units, the Army Medical Corps, the Army Ordinance Corps and the Army Service Corps (except the aforementioned Mechanical Transport specialists). They must have enjoyed a notable income during the months of August and September 1914 but the rate was reduced to one shilling per recruit on 20 October 1914. In any case, there was every incentive for recruiters to use imaginative methods to maximise their income. Some of their methods are examples of military humour, as practised by old soldiers down the ages. A boy who mistakenly gave his real age might be told to 'clear off and come back tomorrow and see if you are nineteen.'

Apart from the failure of the recruiting sergeant to demand some real and indisputable proof of age from a recruit at the time of enlistment, the failure of many doctors to turn away underage recruits is of almost equal importance. The standard of medical examination at the time of enlistment varied alarmingly. It was not only dependent on time, place and circumstance but also on the quality of the doctors. Some doctors were conscientious and caused bottlenecks; some were merely cavalier; some were overwhelmed and some criminally negligent. Young boys, determined to enlist, would seek out the recruiting centres where the doctors were passing anyone who looked reasonably fit. That is the key to it all. The doctors were required to certify a recruit's *apparent* age. This was the great escape clause which allowed thousands of lads to join up well below the age of nineteen. The Duke of Bedford reached a similar conclusion. He wrote on 6 May 1916:

> the normal age for foreign service is 19 ... the age of a boy who enlisted under the voluntary system is determined by the answer given by him at the moment of attestation. He was told by the recruiting authorities that, whatever his real age may have been, he could only join the Army if he put it down as 19. The blame attaches to the recruiting officers. It is they not the boy recruit who should have known better. But the military authorities have decided to hold these boys to the statement of age they were induced to make at the moment of attestation, and disregard the birth certificates which prove the real age to be under 19, and consequently exempt from foreign service ... [These boys] are sent abroad *when their physique is considered to be equivalent to that of 18 ½* [emphasis added].

In the first rush of enthusiasm during the late summer and early autumn of 1914, a number of doctors had little choice in the matter and performed cursory examinations. Many of them may have been influenced by the not uncommon feeling that the war would soon be over. According to the 'Report of the War Office Committee of Enquiry into Shell-shock', a condition which will be addressed later, one doctor in London processed 400 medical examinations in ten days.[6]

One classic example serves to illustrate the culpability of some doctors. Private John Tucker of the 13th London Regiment wrote that he 'answered the various questions, giving a fictitious age of nineteen and was sent up to the gallery to await the Medical Officer.' After some time the doctor made a brief appearance, evidently the better for a bibulous lunch. 'I took off my jacket,' says Tucker, who was then instructed to hold out his arms and open and close his fingers. This satisfied the doctor, who turned on his heels and left.[7] It is still difficult to see how Private S. Lewis of the East Surrey Regiment, who was apparently twelve years old when he enlisted, could have passed even the most cavalier of medical examinations. He did so and fought on the Somme for six weeks. As far as can be determined, he was the youngest recruit who managed to fool the doctors and go on to active service.

The rules for doctors were not specific enough and this may account for many underage recruits passing their medical examinations. In 1915 the simple medical classification for fitness was:

A. Fit for service at home or abroad.
B. Temporarily unfit for service abroad.
C. Fit for service at home only.
D. Unfit for service at home or abroad.

In March 1916, as a result of the unsatisfactory medical examinations, the classification of men called up for service was made more extensive. There were five main categories with sub-categories:

(1) Fitness for general service.
(2) Fitness for field service at home.
(3) Fitness for garrison service: (a) abroad, (b) at home.
(4) Fitness (a) for labour, such as road-making, entrenching and other works, (b) sedentary work only, such as clerical work.
(5) Unfitness for any military service.[8]

Recruiting rates varied widely throughout the country, with London supplying an unusually high number and the West Country, for example, being somewhat less enthusiastic. The too young were happy to seek out any unit which was trying to make up its quota and was thus less scrupulous. In 1914 J.W. Stephenson, who was underage, failed to fool the Royal Army Ordinance Corps in his home town of Skipton and the Royal Horse Artillery in the neighbouring town of Otley into taking him on. Early in 1915, therefore, he travelled to Keighley, where he was unknown, and managed to enlist in the 3/7th Duke of Wellington's Regiment. Arthur Wandsworth, rejected by his local Bradford Pals, travelled to Leeds, lied about his age and joined their Pals regiment instead.[9]

By 1 September 1914 it became clear that Kitchener, who refused to sanction any move that might slow the rate of recruitment, had tapped a well-spring of enthusiasm, which overwhelmed the recruiting organisation and swamped the army's available resources. Some say he had lost control of the recruiting process. At this time an all-party Parliamentary Recruiting Committee was formed. Its composition was significant. The joint presidents were H.H. Asquith, the Liberal prime minister; Andrew Bonar Law, the leader of the Conservative opposition; and Arthur Henderson, the leader of the Parliamentary Labour Party. Henderson's inclusion is notable because he was well respected by the trade union movement, the co-operation of which Kitchener badly needed. He would have noted that the anti-war Independent Labour Party, headed by Ramsey MacDonald, had issued the following statement, which was a sign that all was not sweetness and light on the left of the political spectrum:

> In our view the operation of a sort of moral press-gang will be incompatible and unjust. We must protest against all attempts to force men into the ranks by withholding assistance from them, or dismissing them from their employment. Much as we detest universal military service ... that plan would be less discreditable than the general hunting and harrying of young men now taking place.[10]

It seems that the Independent Labour Party had detected some unpleasant practices.

The Parliamentary Recruiting Committee's head office was at number 12 Downing Street and it was effectively run by the chief whips of the three parties. The zeal of some of its members helped to harness local party machines and to encourage local government and businesses to intervene positively. The urgent need for temporary accommodation for newly attested recruits was alleviated by local improvisations. There is some dispute as to whether this committee was organised in desperation, with Kitchener's perceived failure to control recruiting, or at his behest in order to ensure more men were recruited. Perhaps *The Times* was being polite when it attributed the formation of the committee to Lord Kitchener who, it said, 'has enquired of the leaders of the great political parties if they would jointly agree that their organisations should give their full co-operation in securing the enlistment of more men.' The committee stated that it:

will appeal to the political associations throughout the country to give general assistance to the work of recruiting; will enlist the sympathies and help of the peers, members of Parliament and Parliamentary candidates; will assist the county recruiting committees in obtaining Parliamentary speakers for public meetings; will publish and issue suitable publications in leaflet and pamphlet form, and will in every possible way work in conjunction with the recruiting agencies.

The committee, through the constituency workers, effectively took control of recruiting.

On 11 September 1914 the height standard for recruits was raised to 5ft 6in, which may have put a brake on the number attesting. By mid-September employment levels increased, helped by government contracts for military material. The loss of so many young men to the army reduced the number available for employment. Increased employment and thus better wages undermined recruiting. The October recruiting returns showed a significant drop in numbers to 136,811. Recruiting picked up in November, reaching 169,862, but dropped again to 117,860 in December. On 23 November 1914 *The Times* reported:

On Saturday and yesterday recruiting appeals were made to gatherings of young men in London and the provinces. Saturday's efforts were directed at crowds which were present at football matches, and the results were grievously disappointing. There appears something about the professional football match spectator which makes the recruiting appeal a failure. At the Chelsea ground Colonel Burn M.P. was one of the speakers. Recruiting sergeants were present – but not a man was induced to join. At other football grounds appeals were made with equal ill-success ... the dismal story of Saturday's recruiting was relieved by one man who volunteered at the Woolwich Arsenal ground.

The article went on to point out that rugby clubs, cricket elevens and rowing clubs throughout the kingdom were pouring men into the ranks. This seems to indicate there was a significant section of British society unresponsive to the call to arms.

An open session of the National Convention of the No-Conscription Fellowship was held at the Memorial Hall in Farringdon Street, London, early in November 1914. It was composed largely of men of military age who heard the Chairman, Clifford Allen, quote excerpts from letters which he had received from various MPs. J.H. Thomas MP had written the following:

> It is amazing to me how some people glibly talk of conscription as if it only has to be introduced to be accepted as a necessary blessing of war ... I know of nothing so calculated to divide the nation, so likely to embarrass the Government, and so certain to be resented by the workers as conscription.

Chares Trevelyan MP stated that he would 'oppose conscription without qualification, in the House of Commons and in the country.' The most significant contribution came from Ramsey MacDonald MP who wrote:

> Conscription must never be regarded as a mere military expedient. It strikes right at the root of conscience and ought never to be imposed upon free citizens who have attained any moral conception of individuality. It, therefore, ought to be opposed in principle.

Ramsey MacDonald was a controversial figure. He was MP for Leicester and leader of the Independent Labour Party. His pacifist attitude had cost him the leadership of his party in 1914 and was to cost him his seat in Parliament in 1918. He was, of course, to become the first ever Labour prime minister from January to November 1923.

In August 1915 Rudyard Kipling wrote a series of articles for the *Daily Telegraph* about a tour he had made of the New Army training camps. With government encouragement the articles were edited and published as a small booklet by Macmillan and Co., London. It was priced sixpence and called *The New Army in Training*. Whilst treating his work with due caution, we know that he had an uncanny ability to understand and empathise with enlisted men. He had a good ear for their moods and expressed them sympathetically. He had visited the huge training base at Aldershot and observed the men on the parade ground and in their tents. Here he writes about their feelings:

> [The soldiers] think it vile that so many unmarried young men who are not likely to be affected by government allowances [exempted from

service] should be so shy about sharing their life. They discuss these young men and their womenfolk by name, and imagine rude punishments for them suited to their known characters ... They stare hard, even in their blue slops, at white-collar, bowler-hatted young men, who by the way, are just learning to drop their eyes under that gaze ... And when they are home on leave, the slack-jawed son of the local shop-keeper, the rising nephew of the big banker, and the dumb and cunning carter's lad receive instruction or encouragement suited to their needs and the nation's ... There is a gulf already opening between those who have joined and those who have not; but we will not know the width and depth of that gulf till the war is over. The wise youth is he who jumps in now and lands safely among the trained and armed men.[11]

Kipling's purpose was obvious. Recruiting was slowing down and he was drawing attention to the many able-bodied young men still not in uniform. His point, and that of the men to whom he spoke, is made clear when we look at the figures. By 15 August 1915 a National Register had been taken and the details of every man between eighteen and forty-one were entered on a 'Pink Form'. It is noted here that the 'Pink Forms' of men in reserved occupations were marked with a black star and they were thus called 'Starred Men'. The register, when finally complete, showed that 5,012,146 men of military age were not in the forces, and that of these 2,179,231 were single. Of the single men, only 690,138 were in starred occupations.[12]

In September 1915 only 71,617 men enlisted, despite the publicity and pressure surrounding the National Register. This was the lowest number so far and it coincided with the terrible losses incurred in the Battle of Loos. Kitchener was now concerned enough to report to the cabinet that he needed around 35,000 recruits per week to keep existing units in the BEF up to strength. He now favoured the setting of targets for each recruiting district. Asquith was also concerned but not enough to come down in favour of compulsory service. He appointed Lord Derby, who was a supporter of conscription, as the director general of recruiting on 5 October 1915.

The pressure to produce results led to unforeseen but serious injustices, among which was the enlistment of numerous boy soldiers. Letters of protest began appearing in *The Times*, such as this one, dated 13 August 1915, from E.C. Sparrow of Watford:

Sir – You are fully justified in your criticism of the veiled compulsion now being carried out under the name of voluntary enlistment, and I feel compelled to write to you, as no doubt many others are, to supply evidence of the grave carelessness and worse which appears to be inseparable from the present system. From the south-western half of this county ten consumptives actually under treatment have been accepted, some with gross disease. If this is possible, how many men in an incipient and latent stage, not actually conscious of being ill, must there be present in the armies in the stress and haste which undoubtedly led it scamping [sic] of the medical examination. Another point; A boy lately enlisted from the Urban Council offices here aged only 15 years six months! And I am told by a responsible member of the staff that the recruiting sergeants at a recent 'rally' were trying to persuade boys of 16 to put their ages down as above the limit. On the other hand I can give several instances of young men – three chauffeurs amongst them – who have not yet made any attempt to pass the Army doctor. What is the real reason that our Coalition Cabinet will not give a clear and unanimous call to the nation to fulfil the first duty of every citizen?

This parliamentary exchange of 22 September 1915, though riddled with rhetoric, indicates that some MPs, at least, were seriously concerned about the problem:

Sir A Markham asked the Under-Secretary for War whether he is aware that Private G Jones, No 18731, 11th Devonshire Regiment, sailed for France on 6 October on his fourteenth birthday; will he say what steps the Secretary of State for war proposes taking, if any, to prevent boys of thirteen years of age enlisting against the wishes of their parents ... Are we to understand it is the policy of the Government to take immature boys of fifteen and sixteen when they have set down a definitive military age at which boys may be enlisted? The question has been raised time after time and we get no satisfaction from the Government. Surely no system of enlistment can be satisfactory which allows boys like that to be taken. The War Office well knows that the declarations made by these boys – made for patriotic reasons – are false. I am told that these young boys are unable to stand the fatigue of a campaign and many of them have to return from the War after the country has been put through the expense of training them.

Sir F. Banbury is recorded as saying:

> I suppose they said they were over eighteen. There are many cases where
> recruits under age have been accepted. My Honourable and Gallant Friend
> (Captain Guest) tells me that the age limit already has been rescinded.
> Let me give another case, not within my personal knowledge but told to
> me by a friend who is a general in command of a division and whom I
> have known all my life. I should take what he told me as being a strict fact.
> He informed me that in his division a large number of young boys were
> being sent. These were passed by the civilian doctors and subsequently
> rejected by the military doctors. They had to be sent back home again.[13]

Sir Arthur Markham was a coal mine owner and Liberal MP for
Macclesfield from 1900 to 1916. It is as well to remember that he was
a friend of Lloyd George. He was often found fighting injustice, as he
saw it, and sometimes took risks. He was sued for libel by Wernher
Beit and Co. in 1901, having repeated in public some accusations he
had previously made under parliamentary privilege. He did not like
Kitchener and was active in the attempt to censure him in a debate in
Parliament on 1 June 1916.

By September 1915 Kitchener had begun unilaterally to apply direct
and forceful pressure on local recruiting committees. Here is one
characteristic exchange, this time between the War Office and the Bristol
Recruiting Committee, beginning thus: 'Falling off of recruiting has
caused Lord Kitchener and the War Office great concern.' The Bristol
Committee asked for clarification and was told: 'The battalions, reserves
and other units in your district are 8,000 under establishment. Your
most earnest endeavours to raise men to make up this deficiency are
requested and will be much appreciated.'[14] Such communication would
have caused some consternation and might have led to some extra zeal
being shown by recruiting sergeants, and a calculated reduction in the
vigilance of the medical examiners. The resources directed at recruiting
were growing as the need for volunteers increased. This is illustrated in
an article about a monster recruiting rally, which appeared in *The Times*
of 4 October 1915:

> ... there was plenty of stirring music. Several speeches were made by
> soldiers and members of Parliament. Above all there was a fine display

of young men in khaki … Five columns of Regulars and Territorials each 1,000 strong, and accompanied by bands, starting from five different centres, north, south, east and west … The 50 miles covered altogether embraced within a huge circle all the chief residential and shopping districts of outer London … 'Wake up London' was the motto of the rally. It caused a great stir everywhere. The decline in recruiting of late has been attributed to the slow, drab, and uninspiring trench warfare. But it was impossible not to notice that the crowds on the footways were composed mainly of elderly men and women and children.

Accompanying each column were swarms of recruiting sergeants, wearing red, white and blue rosettes and streamers. They pushed their way through the spectators, casting glances right and left. Not a single young man in the comparatively few in the crowd was overlooked. As each one was approached the soldiers in the march who were in a most boisterous humour shouted 'fall in' and laughed and cheered. The immediate outcome from the rally was, therefore, somewhat meagre. The reports from various recruiting stations on Saturday night were that the response was as normal.

After the dreadful slaughter during the Battle of Loos, which took place between 25 September and 8 October 1915, it became clear to many politicians that the only way to win the war was to increase the size of the British Army. A number of cabinet ministers, hitherto against conscription, were now persuaded that it was necessary, as was Kitchener. Nine of them asked him to persuade Asquith to introduce it but the prime minister saw the move as an attempt to ease him out of office. The casualties at Loos had been so severe that there were not enough men volunteering to keep the divisions up to strength so, in a last-ditch attempt to postpone conscription, Kitchener and Lord Derby, the director general of recruiting, devised the Derby Scheme.

This was a compromise aimed at placating both those in favour of conscription and those in favour of volunteering. All men between the ages of eighteen and forty-one were invited to attest, that is agree to volunteer, when their year was called up. That meant that each man was to be asked face to face either to join up at once or attest to his willingness to join up when summoned. The volunteers were to be divided into forty-six groups, twenty-three of which were to be unmarried men divided up according to their age, and a second twenty-three, similarly divided according to age, of married men whose categories would be called after all the single men had joined the colours. A volunteer under this scheme was given a medical examination and allowed to join the colours immediately, if he so wished. If not, he was sent home to await the call-up of his category. Each category was to be given fourteen days notice to allow the men time to settle their affairs. Lord Derby was instructed by the prime minster and Lord Kitchener to produce 500,000 men by 31 March 1916. It was agreed that conscription would be introduced if the required number of volunteers was not forthcoming using the Derby Scheme.

Lord Derby invited the Parliamentary and Joint Labour Recruiting Committees, together with a number of military officers, to 12 Downing Street for an urgent conference on 15 October 1915 and they hammered out a plan for a new recruiting drive. Lord Derby made this statement after the meeting:

> ... In the past recruits have been found by the military authorities assisted by civilians. I propose to make civilians responsible to bring the raw material in the shape of recruits to the military to enlist, clothe, equip, and train. This can only be rendered possible if some thoroughly representative civilian body be willing to make itself responsible for the work, and my most grateful thanks to the two bodies, the Parliamentary Recruiting Committee and the Joint Labour Recruiting Committee, who have together made themselves jointly responsible ... the manner of dealing with the canvassing is somewhat similar to that which takes place at a General Election, but instead of one party canvassing against another we shall have the unique spectacle of all parties combining to canvass for one common object ... that of obtaining a sufficient number of recruits under the voluntary system to maintain our Armies in the field at the required strength ... The number of units supplied by any particular area, the men needed to bring them up to strength, and, further the men needed to keep them up to strength, will be supplied to the local recruiting committee in order that they may see what is expected of their area, and, I hope, stimulate local patriotism ...

The whole of the work was to be completed by 30 November 1915. In fact, the final date for completion was put back until 15 December 1915. Each un-starred man received a letter from Lord Derby urging him to attest and tribunals were set up to hear claims for exemption. Civic and municipal authorities were co-opted into the scheme and the organisation at local level was extensive. On 15 November 1915 the *Glasgow Herald* carried an advertisement which read:

> Enlist before 30th November. If you do not the Prime Minster has pledged himself and his Government that compulsory means will be taken.

On the same day Lord Kitchener telegraphed the following to the Mayor of Leicester:

> At this critical moment your most earnest efforts in the work of obtaining recruits will be appreciated. We confidently believe that Leicester men … will do their duty and help maintain in the field the high tradition of the men of your borough …[15]

When central government sets targets and marshals the political machines of all parties towards their conclusion, local authorities tend to employ creative methods in meeting them. The pressure would have been transmitted to recruiters who may well have encouraged underage recruits to join up.

The Derby Scheme contained a special clause to deal with the boy soldier. It had been decided that youths of eighteen years of age, who wished to enlist, would receive a day's pay. They would then be held in reserve until they were nineteen. It was acknowledged that strong youths of seventeen and eighteen, who declared themselves to be nineteen and looked it, would probably get into uniform. The under secretary of state for war, Mr Tennant, replied to a parliamentary question about underage recruits as follows:

> If a recruit enlists who has declared his age to be over 19, but who is actually below that age, the War Office do not consider that to be sufficient cause in itself for discharging him from the Army. Under the existing arrangements a soldier who is actually below 19 may be sent abroad provided his physique is considered by the medical authorities to be that of a man of 18 ½ . If his physique is below that of a man of 18 ½ he is retained for training and service at home until he reaches the required standard. In practice the War Office always allows a lad who is under 17 to

be discharged provided application is made to his commanding officer whilst he is serving at home. In the case of soldiers serving overseas, the question of discharge or return to this country rests with the Commander in Chief.[16]

This was the official government position on underage recruits and it was open to wide interpretation, especially by doctors. It amounts to an acknowledgement that the War Office was aware of their presence in the army and intended to take no action itself to seek them out.

At first the Derby Scheme met with some success. The face-to-face canvass and all the propaganda resulted in a flood of men at the recruiting offices, which were once more overwhelmed by the numbers at their doors. However, by the end of the scheme, Lord Derby calculated that only 343,386 single men had enlisted out of an estimated 651,160. This was well below his target. He said that it was not possible to call up the married men until the single men, who had not enlisted, were obtained by other means.

By March 1916 it had become clear that around 1.4 million recruits would be needed immediately if they were to be ready for the expected campaigns in September. Since four months was the absolute minimum training period for an infantryman, it was essential to get them onto the parade grounds without delay.

This meant conscription. It finally came in January 1916, bringing its own burden of injustices. It also forever changed the relationship between the British people and their government. By December 1916, Asquith had been displaced as prime minister by David Lloyd George.

1. One of the playing fields of England. Perhaps the Great War was won on playing fields like this. (*Chris Widdows*)

2. A great imperialist. Public school headmasters, like Eppstein, were responsible for the spread of imperialist propaganda and of the great lie – *Dulce et decorum est pro patria mori.* (*Chris Widdows*)

3. The imperialist's lieutenants. Eppstein's staff were mostly Oxbridge men who preached a brand of muscular Christian imperialism. Their influence was crucial in the development of the hero cult and the games cult. (*Chris Widdows*)

4. The imperialist's stage. Public schoolboys attended chapels like this every day – and twice on Sundays. It was the platform from which muscular Christian imperialism was launched and religion was harnessed to war. (*Chris Widdows*)

5. School for Sacrifice. The Reading School OTC *circa* 1905. After the Boer War debacle, British public schools started to prepare their boys for war. The uniforms in this picture are of the Boer War era and the boys are carrying Lee-Metford rifles. (*Chris Widdows*)

6. Some of the cadets were very young indeed. It was difficult enough for a grown man to tote a Lee-Metford rifle. Some of these boys were not much bigger than the weapon they carried. (*Chris Widdows*)

BISLEY TEAM 1902.

7. The OTC Bisley team. The dreadful state of marksmanship during the Boer War led to an effort to train public schoolboys to shoot. It became competitive, of course, and shooting matches against other public schools took place at the Bisley ranges. This is a picture of a school shooting team of eight boys with their instructors. (*Chris Widdows*)

8. Training for Arm. In addition to basic training, cadet corps were given specialist instruction. This rare picture, taken around 1905, shows Royal Engineer cadets at summer camp learning how to build bridges. (*Chris Widdows*)

9. The arch imperialist himself. Lord Roberts of Kandahar, President of the National Service League, visits Reading School in 1906 as part of his effort to promote his cause. His private aim was to persuade the government to introduce conscription. (*Chris Widdows*)

10. The dangerous year. The Reading School OTC in 1914. So many of these innocent lives were brutally curtailed in the Great War killing fields. (*Chris Widdows*)

11. Flannelled Fools. The Reading School cricket XI of 1914. The stories of some of these young men are told in Chapter 6: School for Sacrifice. (*Chris Widdows*)

12. Muddied Oafs. The Reading School Rugby team, 1914. Four members of this team, W.M. Cooper, C.J. Fuller, D.J. Davis and L.C. Shore were killed in the war. A.P. Avilne MC, and Sgt W.L. Pauer MM and Bar, DCM, were wounded. Of the others, A.H. Bull was a second lieutenant in the army, H.B. Preece was in the Royal Navy, R.F. McIlroy was a sapper and B.H. Churchill won the MC and *Croix de Guerre*. Incidentally, G. Davos was a Belgian refugee who went home to join the Belgian Artillery as a second lieutenant. (*Chris Widdows*)

13. Lord Kitchener of Khartoum. He has been much criticised but his reputation was enormous in 1914. His influence was largely responsible for raising a mass army of 2.5 million volunteers. (*Author's collection*)

14. When the Germans invaded Belgium, a number of posters were produced to promote anti-German feelings and to help the recruiting drive. This is one of them. It shows the signatories of the 1813 treaty which guaranteed the independence and neutrality of Belgium – which, of course, the Germans breached. (*Author's collection*)

15. Germanophobia – Artists 'impressions' like this appeared in British newspapers to arouse hate and anger. (*Author's collection*)

16. Patriotism. A recruiting rally in London. One of many which stirred the blood and turned the heads of thousands of adolescent males. (*Author's collection*)

17. Recruiting fever. The London recruiting offices were overwhelmed with volunteers when Kitchener called for his 'first 100,000'. The rush was so difficult to deal with that numerous underage recruits were able to avoid close scrutiny and join the army. (*Author's collection*)

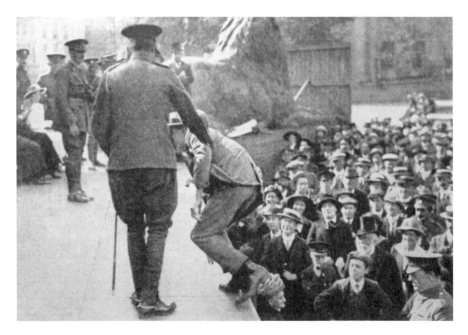

18. Hauling them in. A recruit is helped up to the stage during a recruiting rally. It is clear that most of those in the audience are too old to fight. (*Author's collection*)

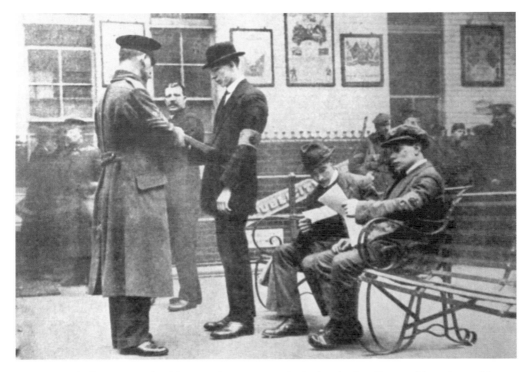

19. Which regiment should I join? A young man in the bowler hat discusses his options with a recruiting sergeant. Note the khaki arm bands to indicate that the men had already attested; they were to protect them from the girls who were presenting the white feather of cowardice to young men in civilian clothes. (*Author's collection*)

20. Attestation. An officer prepares to attest recruits in a town hall somewhere in England. This was the moment when the recruit swore that he was nineteen years of age and eligible to volunteer. No proof of age was required. (*Author's collection*)

21. Lord Derby, Director General of Recruiting and author of the Derby Scheme (*right*). Kitchener likened him to a feather cushion because he showed the imprint of the last person to sit on him. The Scheme failed and conscription was brought in. (*Author's collection*)

22. The Derby Scheme resulted in another recruiting rush. (*Author's collection*)

23. Off to war. Newly recruited men being marched off to begin their training. (*Author's collection*)

24. Gentlemen rankers, of the Artists Rifles, training in a London churchyard. Some have uniforms. Middle-class men rushed into the army in the early years of the war. (*Author's collection*)

25. A Sunday outing. Londoners watch new recruits drilling in the London parks in the summer of 1914. (*Author's collection*)

26. Children watch the recruits drill in a park. Their innocence and optimism was to be short lived. (*Author's collection*)

27. Training. Rapid
fire practice under
realistic conditions.
(*Author's collection*)

28. Training.
Learning to fire
machine guns.
(*Author's collection*)

29. Kitchener's Blues.
A rare picture of
a squad of trainees
wearing the famous
Kitchener's Blues.
These were issued
because there were
not enough uniforms
in store in the first
months of training.
(*Author's collection*)

30. At first, accommodation was in short supply and the majority of volunteers lived under canvass. The hut-building programme was beset by problems. The late summer of 1914 was fine and tented camps were pleasant places to live in. (*Author's collection*)

31. Officers training to be snipers. (*Author's collection*)

32. King George V takes the salute at a passing out parade of New Army infantrymen.
(*Author's collection*)

33. Reality. The Second Battle of Ypres when so many young men lost their lives.
(*Author's collection*)

34. British POWs. Their plight is often overlooked. There were many complaints about the treatment they received. (*Author's collection*)

35. A land fit for heroes? The boys who had joined the new armies straight from school had no work experience. They got very little help. This picture shows some ex-soldiers training to work on the land. (*Author's collection*)

36. They shall not grow old. The Great War memorial in Reading School chapel. (*Chris Widdows*)

37. Lt Col N. Jouques OBE lays a wreath on the Kendrick Boys' War Memorial on Remembrance Sunday 2004. The memorial has the words *Dulce et Decorum est Pro Patria Mori* carved on it. (*Chris Widdows*)

5

TRAINING FOR ARMAGEDDON

What's the use of worrying?
It never was worth while,
So, pack up your troubles in your old kit-bag,
And smile, smile, smile.

George Asaf.

As the twentieth century progressed, criticising Kitchener's new armies became a popular activity. Corelli Barnett, for example, is particularly scathing when he writes:

at every level, from divisional commanders to subalterns, there were inexperienced and ill-trained officers hastily promoted. The staff, crammed on short courses, could not be compared to the professionals on the German staff. Tactics were thus modified because the General-Staff perceived the idea that half-trained troops were incapable of tactical use of ground in small groups and could only be used in a parade ground advance in rigid lines. The slaughter of 60,000 British soldiers in one day on the 1st July 1916 can partly be attributed to this misconception.[1]

When Kitchener began to train his new armies, he was forced to call on Boer War and even pre-Boer War regulars brought out of retirement. These gentlemen were dubbed 'Dug Outs' and some were not up to the task. One critic, Corelli Barnett again, has called them 'the products of the Duke of Cambridge's Army ... too often Colonel Blimps, Sergeant Blimps and Corporal Blimps.' They were said to have been totally out of touch with modern weapons, tactics, organisation and methods. Junior officers and non-commissioned officers had to train on the job.

Of course they were out of touch but many eventually overcame their inadequacies. Here is Pte James Hall explaining how it was done in practice:

> Frequent changes were made in methods of training in England, to correspond with changing conditions of modern warfare as exemplified in the trenches. Textbooks on military tactics and strategy, which were the inspired gospel of the last generation of soldiers, became obsolete overnight. Experience gained in Indian Mutiny wars or on the *veldt* in South Africa was of little value in the trenches in Flanders. The emphasis shifted from open fighting to trench warfare, and the textbook which our officers studied was a typewritten serial issued semiweekly by the War Office, and which was based on the dearly bought experience of officers at the front.

Of trained staff officers, there were virtually none. This was critical; running a headquarters in modern warfare is a complex task. The Germans were sure that the British would be unable to take the field with their new armies because of the lack of staff officers. Theirs, of course, were highly trained and effective.

There are four points to make here. The first is that Kitchener had little choice in the matter. The majority of the trained and experienced regular army officers and NCOs had been sent to France with the BEF and not a few had been killed. However, he managed to keep some in hand to the benefit of the 1st New Army, despite serious opposition from the fighting front. The British government, that is the politicians, had neglected to foresee the need for a mass army. In particular, the absence of a school for training NCOs was a distinct handicap.

What the government had done was to ensure that a large number of young men had received some training in the Officers' Training

Corps in public schools and universities. Some of the positive and useful things that Kitchener did are often ignored. He quickly recognised the value of the National Rifle Association. Its senior members were given reserve commissions and attached to staffs as brigade majors in charge of musketry training. They knew where to find the marksmen in the country and used them in the vital role of musketry trainers.

The second point is that no one managed to solve the special problems of trench warfare until late in the war and thus everyone was in the same boat. This is a point that the critics rarely make with sufficient force.

The third is that the British commanders managed the new armies with sufficient skill to finally win the crushing victories of 1918. The casualties compare favourably with those of the other armies in the war. What is more, there were no significant mutinies in the new armies as there were in the French and Russian armies. This may have had something to do with the number of volunteers from the upper-working and middle classes, the policy of rotation into and out of the combat zone which allowed rest and recuperation, the relationship between front line officers and men and, in particular, the high level of motivation which was retained despite the dreadful slaughter and discomfort.

The fourth point is that the lack of sufficient officers and NCOs in the early days of the new armies may have allowed the underage soldiers to stay at the front undetected. Indeed, some of the 'Dug Outs' may have approved of their patriotism and encouraged them to stay.

Kitchener insisted that the new armies would be trained as well as possible before they were sent into battle. As we have seen, he was angry when untrained Imperial Yeomen were sent out to fight in South Africa and he was determined that the mistake would not be repeated. The syllabus for the six-month course of training for the new armies was first laid down in Army Order 388 and was followed as closely as circumstances permitted. The 1st Army commenced individual training, including musketry, on 15 August 1914. Company training began on 16 November and ended on 23 December for the Christmas festivities.

By 17 August 1914 training camps had been designated. The 8th (Light) Division and the 9th (Scottish) Division were to train at Aldershot, the 1st Irish Division at Dublin and the Curragh, the 13th Eastern Division at Shorncliffe, Colchester and Rainham, the 13th Western Division on Salisbury Plain. The command of the training centre for the 11th (Northern) Division had not, by that time, been decided.

The organisation was often slow in getting off the ground. The early administrative and logistical failures have focused the attention of a number of influential writers. The errors were irritating and, in hindsight, often avoidable but we should concentrate on the fact that they were resolved in the end and that the volunteer soldiers, who were inconvenienced, managed to improvise and survive well enough. Looked at another way, it might be argued that overcoming difficulties helped to prepare soldiers for the real hardships they were to face in combat. There is no doubt that the intelligence level of the New Army recruits was much higher than that of the old regular army and this made for interesting adjustments in training and discipline. Despite the fact that a significant number of boy soldiers were recruited, the average age of recruits in the early days was higher than that of the regular army.

At Shorncliffe, for example, 700 men of the 8th Royal West Kents, a battalion of the 24th Division, reached camp in the rain on Saturday 12 September 1914 to find that no arrangements had been made to accommodate them. They were marched from the railway station to an open field and told to stay under some trees to keep dry. The situation was so bad that a number of men went home by train. Bell tents were supplied for the remainder on the following Monday. No eating utensils were available for a number of days, so pieces of wood were used for plates.[2]

In the very early days, waste and chaos prevailed. Camps were sited in the wrong places and buildings were erected only to be condemned. The curious political tension surrounding the introduction of the Derby Scheme made its own contribution to the shambles. No plans had been made to accommodate the recruits enlisting under the scheme and, since the numbers it was supposed to raise were not divulged, forward planning became difficult. To add to the problems of hut building, there were frequent labour disputes between contractors and workers, which held up progress considerably. The problems were exacerbated by the breakdown in relations between the War Office and the Amalgamated Society of Carpenters and Joiners at a crucial stage in the hut building programme and the shortage of skilled labour became acute.

Accommodation at Shorncliffe throughout the autumn and winter of 1914–15 was of a makeshift order. Troops slept in leaky tents or hastily constructed wooden shelters. St Martin's Plain, Shorncliffe, was an ideal camping site in the summer but, when the weather broke in mid-October, the land became a quagmire. Late in November the troops were moved to wooden huts at Sandling Junction to make room for newly recruited units. The huts were half-finished, the drains were open ditches and floods became common. Life was wretched until January when billets became available in the Metropole, one of Folkestone's most fashionable hotels.

Rudyard Kipling wrote about life in the training camps in 1915 and carefully gave his readers a taste of the social profile of the New Army.

> The cook-houses, store-rooms, forges and workshops were collections of tilts, poles, rick-cloths and old lumber, beavered together as on service. The officers' mess was a thin soaked marquee. Scattered amongst the tents were rows of half-built tin sheds, the ready-prepared lumber and corrugated iron lying beside them, waiting to be pieced together like child's toys. But there were no workmen. I was told that they had come in the morning but knocked off because it was wet.

Kipling found more problems with the hut building programme at Lark Hill camp where the Canadians were training:

> Hundreds of tin huts are being built there, but leisurely, by contractors. I noticed three workmen at 11 o'clock that Monday forenoon, as drunk as Davey's sow, reeling and shouting across the landscape.

Tented camps were the commonest form of accommodation. Living in a bell tent could be interesting on a bad night. Overcrowded tents, with twenty-five men trying to undress or dress, proved to be a less than amusing experience. The man who was allotted the space near the entrance had a serious problem. Night latrines were placed just outside the tent-flap. He who needed a pee in the night was forced to climb over the prone figures of his mates, lurch out to the latrine, relieve himself and lurch back into the tent to find his place again. The problem would have been more acute after a boozy night. Men have a propensity to make navigational errors in such circumstances.

Here is Kipling again in an atmospheric piece of writing:

> But when grousing gets beyond a certain point – say at three a.m., in steady wet, with the tent-pegs drawing like false teeth – the nephew of

the insurance agent asks the cousin of the baronet to inquire of the son of the fried-fish vendor what the stevedore's brother and the tutor of the public school joined the Army for. Then they sing 'Somewhere the Sun is shining' till the Sergeant Ironmonger's assistant cautions them to drown in silence or the Lieutenant Telephone-appliances-manufacturer will speak to them in the morning.

Tons of food was purchased overseas, only to be thrown away. The government was robbed by some hotel-keepers, who made absurd claims for damages done to their property by billeted troops. But as the months passed, there was a marked change for the better. The distribution of supplies, the housing and equipping of troops and their movements from one training area to another were greatly improved. Despite the early problems, the food supply was always adequate and often far better than that which many poor civilians were able to command. Peter Simkins tells the story of Richard Patterson, who enlisted in the 1st City of London Rifles at the age of fifteen and who was, at first, billeted in a school near his regiment's drill hall in Farringdon. Patterson stated that

> after meal times, a crowd of hungry children would gather outside the school with bowls and dishes and line up for left-overs dispensed by the cooks. They had a grand treat, he said, when the meal had been stew.[3]

That there were not enough uniforms available for the large number of new recruits is painfully obvious and has been well chewed over by commentators. Images of soldiers of the new armies training in their ragged civilian clothes have become almost a cliché. The deficiencies were made up by improvisation. Post Office uniforms were used and blue slops –called 'Kitchener's Blues' – were run up quickly. Eventually Kitchener issued orders which allowed commanders to make local purchases and many were the improvised results. One eyewitness account of the early days is worth quoting at length:

> We declined to accept the responsibility for the seeming slowness of our progress. We threw it unhesitatingly upon the War Office, which had not equipped us in a manner befitting our new station in life. Although we were recruited immediately after the outbreak of war, less than half of our number had been provided with uniforms. Many still wore their old

civilian clothing. Others were dressed in canvas fatigue suits, or the worn-out uniforms of policemen and tramcar conductors. Every old-clothes shop on Petticoat Lane must have contributed its allotment of cast-off apparel.

Our arms and equipment were of an equally nondescript character. We might easily have been mistaken for a mob of vagrants which had pillaged a seventeenth-century arsenal. With a few slight changes in costuming for the sake of historical fidelity, we would have served as a citizen army for a realistic motion-picture drama depicting an episode in the French Revolution.

We derived what comfort we could from the knowledge that we were but one of many battalions of Kitchener's first hundred thousand equipped in this same makeshift fashion. We did not need the repeated assurances of cabinet ministers that England was not prepared for war. We were in a position to know that she was not. Otherwise, there had been an unpardonable lack of foresight in high places. Supplies came in driblets. Each night, when parades for the day were over, there was a rush for the orderly room bulletin board, which was scanned eagerly for news of an early issue of clothing. As likely as not we were disappointed, but occasionally jaded hopes revived.

'Number 15 platoon will parade at 4 P.M. on Thursday, the 24th, for boots, puttees, braces, and service dress caps.'

Number 15 is our platoon. Promptly at the hour set we halt and right-turn in front of the Quartermaster Stores marquee. The quartermaster is there with pencil and notebook, and immediately takes charge of the proceedings.

'All men needing boots, one pace step forward, March!'

The platoon, sixty-five strong, steps forward as one man.

'All men needing braces, one pace step back, March!'

Again we move as a unit. The quartermaster hesitates for a moment; but he is a resourceful man and has been through this many times before. We all need boots, quite right! But the question is, who needs them most? Undoubtedly those whose feet are most in evidence through worn soles and tattered uppers. Adopting this sight test, he eliminates more than half the platoon, whereupon, by a further process of elimination, due to the fact that he has only sizes 7 and 8, he selects the fortunate twelve who are to walk dry shod.

The same method of procedure is carried out in selecting the braces. Private Reynolds, whose trousers are held in place by a wonderful mechanism composed of shoe-laces and bits of string, receives a pair; likewise, Private Stenebras, who, with the aid of safety pins, has fashioned coat and trousers into an ingenious one-piece garment. Caps and puttees are distributed with like impartiality, and we dismiss, the unfortunate ones growling and grumbling in discreet undertones until the platoon commander is out of hearing, whereupon the murmurs of discontent become loudly articulated.[4]

A typical training day for a New Army infantry battalion is described by Pte James Norman Hall as follows:

> For an hour before breakfast we did Swedish drill, a system of gymnastics which brought every lazy and disused muscle into play. Two hours daily were given to musketry practice. We were instructed in the description and recognition of targets, the use of cover, but chiefly in the use of our rifles. Through constant handling they became a part of us, a third arm which we grew to use quite instinctively. We fired the recruit's, and later, the trained soldier's course in musketry on the rifle ranges … gradually improving our technique, until we were able to fire with some accuracy, fifteen rounds per minute. When we had achieved this difficult feat, we ceased to be recruits … After musketry practice, the remainder of the day was given to extended order, company, and battalion drill. Twice weekly we route-marched from ten to fifteen miles; and at night, after the parades for the day were finished, boxing and wrestling contests, arranged and encouraged by our officers, kept the red blood pounding through our bodies until 'lights out' sounded at nine o'clock.

Battalion training began on 27 December 1914 and finished on 14 January 1915. Brigade training was from 15–31 January. Divisional training was scheduled for 1–15 February. Here is Pte Hall describing the changes he experienced in his training schedule:

> The character of our training changed as we progressed. We were done with squad, platoon, and company drill. Then came field maneuvers [sic]. There were attacks in open formation upon entrenched positions, finishing always with terrific bayonet charges. There were mimic battles, lasting all day, with from ten to twenty thousand men on each side. Artillery, infantry, cavalry, aircraft – every branch of army service,

in fact – had a share in these exciting field days when we gained bloodless victories or died painless and easy deaths at the command of red-capped field judges. We rushed boldly to the charge, shouting lustily, each man striving to be first at the enemy's position, only to be intercepted by a staff officer on horseback, staying the tide of battle with uplifted hand.

The frequent criticism levied at the New Army's training for trench warfare is unfair, or based upon a failure to study the available evidence. A report on the training at Salisbury, in December 1915, revealed that extensive and realistic trenches had been dug on the Plain, in which trainees were given practice in both defence and attack and in which overnight acclimatisation training took place.

The selection and training of officers in the new armies was not without its critics. A summary of events was made in June 1916 by Spencer Wilkinson, Professor of Military History at Oxford, who stated that at the beginning of the war, from August 1914 to the winter, there was a great rush of educated young men for commissions, which were mostly given to suitable candidates who then joined their battalions and were well or ill trained in accordance with the traditions of the battalion and the degree of competence of its commanding officer. In that period thousands of young public school and university men, many of whom had served in the Officers' Training Corps, joined the Territorial Battalions or the new regular army. In the new regular battalions training was very unequal, good commanding officers paying a great deal of attention to it, others confining themselves to old-fashioned drill and orderly-room work.

As more battalions were raised, a period of chaos ensued. Commissions were given with less judgement than at first and instruction of the greater number accepted was unsatisfactory. In the third phase, schools of instruction were founded and young officers sent to them, usually for short courses of a few weeks. Later, the War Office regulated the general courses and laid down that no officer should go to the front unless he passed an examination in discipline, drill, musketry, tactics and field warfare, topography and trench warfare, billeting, machine guns, interior economy and military law, physical drill and signaling.

Wilkinson's observations led him to believe that the results were not satisfactory, so he suggested that Officers' Training Corps should be established where basic and leadership training could occur before commissioning, after which training in musketry, machine guns, signaling and so on could take place in specialist schools. There is no evidence that Wilkinson's suggestions were implemented but it must be said in this context that the contribution of the school and university OTCs cannot be underestimated.

Once training was completed, the move to the front began. Aldershot was the centre where so many were prepared for their last journey from England. There they received an overseas haircut, which, like the US Army crew cut during the Second World War, was very short to reduce the habitat for fleas and head lice.

Kitchener's famous letter was distributed to each soldier. It read:

You are ordered abroad as a soldier of the King to help our French comrades against an invasion of a common enemy. You have to perform a task which will need your courage, your energy, your patience. Remember that the honour of the British Army depends upon your individual conduct. It will be your duty not only to set an example of discipline and perfect steadiness under fire, but also to maintain the most friendly relations with those whom you are helping in this struggle. The operations in which you are engaged will, for the most part, take place in a friendly country, and you can do your own country no better service than by showing yourself, in France and Belgium, in the true character of a British soldier.

Be invariably courteous, considerate, and kind. Never do anything likely to destroy property, and always look upon looting as a disgraceful act. You are sure to meet with a welcome and be trusted; and your conduct must justify that welcome and trust. Your duty cannot be done unless your health is sound. So keep constantly on guard against any excesses. In this new experience you may find temptations both in wine and women. You must entirely resist both temptations, and while treating all women with perfect courtesy, you should avoid any intimacy.
Do your duty bravely. Fear God. Honour the King.
Kitchener. F.M.

On the day of embarkation, battalions were drawn up on the Aldershot parade grounds. Every man had his full kit distributed about his body by webbing straps. His rifle was the Short Lee Enfield, Mark IV, and his bayonet was the long single-edged blade in general use throughout the British Army. In addition to his arms, he carried 120 rounds of .303-calibre ammunition, an entrenching tool, a water bottle, a haversack containing both emergency and the day's rations, and his pack, all strapped to his shoulders and waist in such a way that the weight was equally distributed. His pack contained the following articles: a greatcoat, a woolen shirt, two or three pairs of socks, a change of underclothing, a 'housewife' – the soldiers' sewing-kit – a towel, a cake of soap and a hold-all in which were a knife, fork, spoon, razor, shaving-brush, toothbrush and comb. All of these were useful and sometimes essential articles, particularly the toothbrush, which was regarded as the best instrument for cleaning the mechanism of a rifle. Strapped on top of the pack was the blanket-roll wrapped in a waterproof ground sheet and hanging beneath it was the canteen in its khaki-cloth cover. Each man wore an identification disc on a cord around his neck. It was stamped with his name, regimental number, regiment, and religion. A first-aid field dressing, consisting of an antiseptic gauze pad, a bandage and a small vial of iodine, sewn in the lining of his tunic, completed the equipment.

The whole embarkation process was timed precisely. Each battalion was marched to its allotted railway station and loaded into its own train, together with all its logistical, medical and transport support. The train moved off for the port, to be followed in half an hour by another and so on. Each train drew up beside its allotted troop ship – a grey painted liner commandeered from the merchant fleet – and the stevedores loaded stores, draught animals, wagons and ammunition with precise and practised skill. Within half an hour the battalion was off its train and on the ship and the next train had arrived. As night fell, ship after ship made for the sea and was picked up by its Royal Navy escort of two destroyers, one on each side, to guard against submarine attack.

The overnight trip to France was usually uneventful and on arrival the precise routine of disembarkation began. Each battalion was loaded into its own French Army troop train and commenced a slow journey through the Norman countryside to a station some twenty miles or so from the front. The British Army Service Corps had all but taken over the countryside for its ammunition dumps, vehicle parks, blacksmiths' shops, field kitchens, field hospitals and motor repair shops. London buses, painted grey, shunted troops about.

On arrival at their destination, the battalions disembarked from their trains and marched the last long miles to the fighting front. The roads were cobbled and hard to walk on. This took its toll and, whereas route marches of twenty miles were the norm in England, in France stages were reduced to nine miles and battalions bivouacked for the night in makeshift camps. Many older men began to show fatigue and some even died of it. Eventually the noise of the guns was heard and guides met the marching columns. The guides directed them through the maze of support trenches to the combat trenches, where they met the experienced men who would give them a twenty-four-hour familiarisation course on being at the front.

This was a vital crash course, during which the new men were under fire and within speaking distance of the enemy. They learnt about rats, bugs, lice, latrines, snipers, and mud. They learnt about shaving in leftover tea and how to sleep five men in a 4ft by 6ft dugout. They learnt how machine guns were sighted, how to tell where a German sniper might be, how bombing parties went out in the night to throw grenades into the German trenches and what it was like at night with the flares going up. They watched as men were killed and buried behind the trenches. They learnt that the Germans were well equipped and fine fighting men. This surprised them because they had been told by ignorant British newspaper columnists that their enemy was scared and could not fight.

They also learnt that enemy snipers, artillerymen, airmen, machine gunners and engineers were constantly seeking to impose their will and win the battle for morale. It was never safe to relax. Shell and shrapnel fire came in at frequent intervals and buried men alive or sent the men to ground, while bits of hot metal whizzed about them. Once they had absorbed all of this and more, they were pitched into battle. However, training did not stop. Battalions were given rest periods, followed by training periods at depots in France, during which skills were honed and lessons learnt.

The modern view of Kitchener's New Army has been hijacked by the peculiar nature and power of television. The untimely death during the First World War of a short-sighted boy of eighteen has received a great deal of attention. Second Lieutenant John Kipling of the 2nd Battalion, the Irish Guards, the only son of Rudyard and Caroline Kipling, was severely wounded and reported missing in action at Chalk Pit Wood at around 5 p.m. on 27 September 1915 during the Battle of Loos. He was one of the many thousands of young public schoolboys who had rushed straight from school into the army and, as we have seen, was by no means unique, but his story helps us follow one schoolboy from the playing fields of Wellington, his school, to the killing fields of Loos.

There is no doubt that the Battle of Loos, fought for strategic purposes, was ill-conceived at a tactical level. Kitchener, British secretary of state for war, Field Marshal Sir John French, the officer in overall charge of the British Army in France, and Douglas Haig, the battle commander, all stand accused of allowing ambition to cloud their judgement by agreeing to launch the attack, which they knew would lead to terrible losses. On 21 September 1915 the thirteen divisions of the British Expeditionary Force, at the behest and in support of the fifty-four French divisions, commenced a heavy artillery offensive on the German lines about the small mining town of Loos in Artois. On 25 September Haig launched an infantry attack, which he supported with the release of chlorine gas. Some of the gas blew back upon the British, poisoning 2,632 men and killing seven. The well-defended and entrenched Germans were astonished to see the British massed infantry attacking as though on parade. They cut them down in their thousands with withering machine-gun fire. The slaughter was so great that the Germans stopped firing at the retreating survivors.

At the insistence of Sir John French, the reserve divisions, on which Haig's battle plan depended to save the day, had been held for too long and were too far behind the battle zone. Among them was John Kipling with 2nd Battalion the Irish Guards, which had recently arrived in France. He wrote this to his father on 20 August 1915:

> Here we are billeted in a splendid little village some twenty miles from the firing line. The idea is I believe that we stay here about a fortnight before we go up to the trenches ...

To reach Loos they had to march for hours, footslogging in full kit, mostly by night to avoid aerial observation. John Kipling wrote to his father again, this time on 23 September:

> Just a hurried line to let you know what we are doing. We have begun what I said we were going to do; have been marching for the last two days ...

The night before he moved off for his fatal battle, John Kipling wrote in
a letter home:

> Just a hurried line as we start off tonight. The front line trenches are
> nine miles off from here so it won't be a very long march … The guns
> have been going deafeningly all day, without a single stop. We have to
> push through at all costs so we won't have much time in the trenches,
> which is great luck … We marched 18 miles last night in pouring wet. It
> came down in sheets steadily … You have no idea what enormous efforts
> depend on the next few days … This will be my last letter most likely for
> some time … Well so long dears.
> Dear love John.

Around eighty per cent of the British attacking force was either killed
or wounded during the Battle of Loos. Of this dreadful battle, Ernst
Junger wrote:

> here chivalry disappeared for always. Like all noble and personal
> feelings it had to give way to the new tempo of battle and to the rule of
> the machine.[5]

Carrie Kipling wrote to a relative who had admired her courage in
allowing her son to go to war:

> one can't let ones friends' and neighbours' sons be killed in order to save
> us and our son. There is no chance that John will survive unless he is so
> maimed from a wound as to be unfit to fight. We know it and he does.
> We all know it, but we must all give and do what we can and live on the
> shadow of a hope that our boy will be the one to escape.[6]

This is quite revealing – recent films and writings suggest that John
Kipling's death occurred because his famous father had wangled a
commission for him in the Irish Guards when he was a boy of seventeen.

John Kipling wanted to volunteer as an officer at the age of seventeen,
as was perfectly legal, and as did so many of his contemporaries, and he
had asked his father to support him. He made a number of attempts,
which were rebuffed because of his poor eyesight. In this he was not
alone. A number of young men with poor eyesight used stratagems to

pass the medical examination. One applicant for a commission, Morris Bickersteth, memorised the letters and numbers on the eyesight test card at Aitchison's, the opticians in Leeds, before presenting himself for his examination. Fortunately for him, he was required to read an identical card. He was passed fit for service and granted a commission in the Leeds Pals. George Eyston managed to pass the medical for the University and Public School Brigade by trying to memorise the eye test card whilst the doctor was absent from the room. In the event, he could only remember the top and bottom lines. This appeared to satisfy the doctor who, though exasperated by the apparent anomaly, gave it up as a bad job and passed him fit for service.[7]

John Kipling may well have abandoned the idea but, instead, sought his father's aid. Rudyard asked his friend Field Marshal Lord Roberts, the colonel-in-chief of the Irish Guards, to overlook the eyesight problem and nominate John for a commission in his own regiment. By September 1914 he was a subaltern training with the Guards. When he went home for a short leave on the 28th he impressed his father, who wrote this to Elsie Kipling about him:

> Saturday came John in full canonicals. He very much becomes the uniform ... I am immensely pleased with our boy. The old spirit of carping and criticism has changed into a sort of calm judicial attitude.[8]

John Kipling put in a full period of training with the 2nd Battalion the Irish Guards. On 5 July 1915 he had been on a route march in command of a company. He had marched with the Earl of Kerry, his commanding officer, who told him that he would be the first subaltern to go out to France after his 18th birthday. Kerry had also told him that he would have been too young to go if he had not had a year's service with the brigade. He needed his parents' written permission to go to France and this he obtained. No doubt that, too, came back to haunt Carrie and Rudyard Kipling when he was killed in action.

Of course John's parents felt an overwhelming sense of guilt, just as any parents would have in similar circumstances. Rudyard wrote of his grief in the poem 'My Boy Jack', which inspired the title of the modern novel:

> Have you any news of my boy Jack?
>   *Not this tide,*

When d'you think he'll come back?
  Not with this wind blowing, not this tide ...

Oh, dear, what comfort can I find?
  None this tide,
  Nor any tide,
Except that he did not shame his kind –
Not even with that wind blowing, and that tide.

Rudyard wrote to his friend Brigadier L.C. 'Stalky' Dunsterville on 12 November 1915:

Our boy was reported wounded and missing since September 27th – the Battle of Loos and we have heard nothing official since. But all we can pick up from the main points to the fact that he is dead and probably wiped out by shell fire. However, he had his heart's desire and he didn't have long in the trenches. The Guards advanced on a front of two platoons for each battalion. He led the right platoon over a mile of open ground in the face of shell and machine gun fire and was dropped at the further limit of the advance, after emptying a pistol into a house full of German m.g.'s. His C.O. and his Company Commander told me how he had led 'em and the wounded have confirmed it. He was the senior ensign tho' only 18 yrs and 6 weeks, and worked like the devil at Warley and knew his Irish to the ground. He was reported as one of the best of the subalterns and was a gym instructor and signaller. It was a short life. I'm sorry that all the year's work ended in that one afternoon but – lots of people are in our position – and it is something to have bred a man. The wife is standing it wonderfully tho' she, of course, clings to the bare hope of his being a prisoner. I've seen what shells can do, and I don't.[9]

According to Carrington, some two years after John's death Rudyard's relative, Oliver Baldwin, discovered Sergeant Farrell of the Irish Guards, who had been with Second Lieutenant John Kipling when the leading companies had

forced their way into a gap between Hill Seventy and Hulluch, the deepest penetration made by any British troops in the Battle of Loos. They had fought their way through Chalk-pit wood ... and had encountered strong resistance amongst some houses beyond the wood.

Carrington states that John was using his revolver when he was 'shot through the head and was laid under cover in a shell hole by the Sergeant.' The Guards were driven back by the Germans and it was some time before the ground was recovered by the British.[10] Since the body was not found, John Kipling's name was carved on the memorial to the missing at Loos. At the time of writing, the Commonwealth War Graves Commission had recently announced that John Kipling's remains had been identified and recovered, although some respected historians argue that the remains are not those of John Kipling at all. Once again the problems of identifying the dead and the growth of myth and misinformation hover around the untimely death of a young soldier.

In her novel *Kipling's Choice*, Gert Spillebeen makes a fictionalised John Kipling, a myopic and physically weak boy, serve as a proxy for the thousands of young, eager, yet ill-prepared volunteers sacrificed in the First World War. She appears to imply that his father, the great imperialist, was unduly prominent in perpetrating a grand lie, which sent so many young men to fight and die. She has the bereaved Rudyard Kipling slumped in grief saying 'Why? Did I have to defend that war so strongly? ... How many boys have I written into the grave?'[11] Her description of John Kipling's last moments appears to have made a lasting impact.

> At five o'clock Lieutenant John Kipling is observed for the last time, his head is bloodied and he seems half-crazy, bawling from pain ... he takes a bandage and tries to stop the blood which is running from the shattered remains of his face.

Perhaps the author of these lines had access to later evidence; the scene does not fit in with the story told by Sergeant Farrell and recorded by Carrington. To compound the problem, David Gilmour, in his book *The Long Recessional – The Imperial Life of Rudyard Kipling*, states that John Kipling had 'crawled into a building subsequently occupied by Germans.'[12]

It is likely that the evidence about John Kipling's last moments is being overtaken by a developing myth. It is also possible that Rudyard

Kipling's role in his son's death has been examined with some bias and the conclusion extrapolated beyond what the evidence will bear. For example, *The Sunday Times* of 11 November 2007 carried an article about the letters from John Kipling to his parents which have been gathered together in *O Beloved Kids*, edited by Elliot L. Gilbert, some parts of which I have used and acknowledged above. The letters are valuable and interesting primary evidence, remarkably illustrative of the published military history of the Battle of Loos. They deserve our attention.

The Sunday Times reviewer ventures a few opinions about Rudyard's real grief at the death of his son. Rudyard Kipling, the reviewer suggests, was

> a fervent wartime propagandist whose intervention led his beloved teenage son, John, to die amid the carnage of the trenches.

Both statements are true. By placing the two truths in one sentence, the implications are expanded and a new meaning is given to both. Kipling was, in fact, a propagandist who had warned the British of an impeding war with Germany and made himself unpopular in doing so. To imply that his 'intervention' was the cause of John's death suggests that any action we take to assist our children may have fatal consequences.

The *Independent* published a piece under the headline 'The Great War and its Aftermath: The Son who Haunted Kipling'. It was written to tie in with the dramatisation of *My Boy Jack*. It is a powerful piece but it shows how fiction moves us further along the road to rewriting history. The author writes of John Kipling's death as portrayed in the film:

> Last seen on the second day of the ill-fated attack, stumbling blindly through the mud, screaming in agony after an exploding shell had ripped his face apart ...

He also makes this remark about Rudyard's reaction to his son's death:

> John's death rocked his father's belief in the British military elite, particularly General Haig, who went on to lead the war effort as a result of the battle.

The word 'elite' is here used provocatively. It has class-war overtones. Kipling certainly expressed some strong reservations about the handling of the battle, with reference to the long march of the Irish Guards and their being pitched into battle with insufficient rest. I would suggest that his major criticism was directed at the politicians who allowed Britain to enter the war without due preparation.

The Battle of Loos was a low point in the war and there were to be plenty more before the victories of 1918. The new armies eventually succeeded against the odds and won. There were three main factors which led to their success. The first was the social cohesion which derived from the way the armies were raised. Men from the same street, village, sports club, bank, factory, school, university and town hall volunteered together and stayed together throughout the war. The second was the calibre of junior officers and senior NCOs. These men spent eight hours a day with the sections and platoons they commanded and knew each man well. The third was the unique nature of the private soldiers. They were largely volunteers of high quality who wanted to learn to fight. The discipline was based on mutual support between leaders and those they led. For all their massive size, the Kitchener's new armies were based around cohesive platoons, in which officers and men lived, fed, relaxed, trained and fought together.

SCHOOL FOR SACRIFICE

I am going over the parapet with a shout of 'School' on my lips and then pray God's will be done!

Lieutenant Giles Ayres, 8 May 1915. He was killed the next day.

On 18 June 1914, just before the assassination of Archduke Ferdinand which indirectly led to the First World War, eleven Reading School boys took the field to play the annual match against the gentlemen of the Marylebone Cricket Club. By some accounts, Reading School and the MCC had played cricket against each other nearly every year since the early days of the latter's history, although no proof of this exists at Lord's. In any case, a print dated 1816, of boys playing cricket at Reading School, still hangs on one of the grand staircases in the famous pavilion at Lord's.

It is almost a cliché: a public school cricket match in which a team of schoolboys takes on the mighty MCC during the summer of 1914. Scenes like this have been satirised, criticised and deplored by poets, authors, playwrights and film makers. The whole public school games culture was, to some, the very seat and core of the great lie which was foisted onto a lost generation of lions, who were sacrificed in a useless war by incompetent generals. It has been vilified as the breeding ground of the public school spirit, the hero cult, the muddied oaf and the flannelled fool.

The near mythical picture of early twentieth-century public school-boys playing cricket embodies a vision of imperial manliness, which survived until the dreadful Battle of Loos in September 1915. To be awarded the ribboned coat and tasselled cap for representing the school at sport was seen as a precursor to winning gallantry awards in the field of battle for England and her Empire.

Henry Newbolt, the Old Cliftonian, articulated the vision in his familiar poem about cricket, imperial warfare and public schoolboys:

There's a breathless hush in the Close tonight –
Ten to make and the match to win –
A bumping pitch and a blinding light,
An hour to play and the last man in.
And it's not for the sake of a ribboned coat,
Or the selfish hope of a season's fame,
But his Captain's hand on his shoulder smote –
'Play up! play up! and play the game!'

The sand of the desert is sodden red, –
Red with the wreck of a square that broke; –
The Gatling's jammed and the Colonel dead,
And the regiment blind with dust and smoke.
The river of death has brimmed its banks,
And England far, and Honour a name,
But the voice of a schoolboy rallies the ranks:
'Play up! play up! and play the game!'

This the word that year by year
While in her place the School is set
Every one of her sons must hear,
And none that hears it dare forget.
This they all with a joyful mind
Bear through life like a torch in flame,
And falling fling to the host behind –
'Play up! play up! and play the game!'

Here is the story of a real game of cricket played at the new Reading School on one of the classic playing fields of England. The backdrop was a stereotypical public school building, imperial in concept and designed by the Victorian architect Alfred Waterhouse. Its foundation stone had been laid by the Prince of Wales in 1870 and the school had been opened by the Lord Chancellor, Lord Hatherly, on 11 September 1871.

The match was written up in the *Reading School Magazine* by one of those muscular Christian school masters with a sharp turn of phrase and a deep knowledge of cricket.

READING SCHOOL v MCC.
Played on June 18th and lost by 10 wickets.

This was our first defeat of the season, and it was certainly a very bad beating. But our opponents brought down a side of far more than average strength, which could have easily accounted for any Public School in the country. The absence of Toumlin, also, made a great difference to the batting strength. Clarke, the googly bowler, was at the very top of his form, and was at times quite unplayable. Ambrose, who went in first played a most creditable innings, his driving being particularly good; and his 27 consisted of 6 fours and a three. Shirley and Bardsley, who began confidently, were both out through playing back when they ought to have played forward. Cooper made a blind swipe and paid the natural penalty. Pauer did the same, and of the rest Churchill alone made anything of a stand. The bowlers resolutely refused to put the ball where King's one stroke could hit it, and we were all out for 78.

Our opponents soon knocked off the runs necessary for victory, though Barker was badly missed by King, who ought never to have been put at cover, and then the Rev. Swann-Mason proceeded with great care to make 175. Barker was finely caught by King at mid-off, but no one else was very comfortable with Cooper, who bowled quite well without much luck. Swan-Mason hit 26 fours in a very fine, if rather lengthy innings. The School fielding was, with one or two lapses, quite good throughout, and Churchill kept wicket excellently, stumping 4 men and only giving away 2 byes in an innings of 300.[1]

What happened to those schoolboys who were beaten so emphatically by the gentlemen of the MCC? Ten out of the eleven went to war.

Toumlin, who was clearly missed on the day, volunteered for Kitchener's New Army as a private in the London Rifle Brigade, was wounded in 1916 and captured by the Germans in June 1918.

F.L.M. Shirley, who had captained the team that day, went directly from school to the Royal Military College, Sandhurst, was commissioned as a second lieutenant in the Yorkshire Regiment and seconded to the Royal Flying Corps. In July 1916, by now a trained pilot flying operationally somewhere on the Western Front, he wrote to his old schoolmasters to describe his flight to France:

> We have at last arrived in France after many false alarms as to when we should be ready to go. My trip was not without excitement. We started from Rugby on 15 July and after following the L & N.W.R. as far as London, through a number of storms which cut one's face about, were over Wormwood Scrubs when my engine began to spit and splutter, and as I was wet through I thought it best to come down and have my engine seen to, before attempting the Channel. I had a very good trip to France, but could see very little at 5,500 feet over the channel as the clouds and mist looked very thick … I went over the lines for the first time yesterday afternoon and could plainly see the guns working their havoc. The Huns seem to have a mania for shelling certain woods close round here; trying to cut many of our army of pursuit or reserves, I suppose.

> … we are living in stables, about as cramped as we could be, with a fair amount of comfort … the Hun airman seems to be thoroughly afraid of us. He only comes up when he sees a stranger, and then there are five or six at a time …

Shirley fought a brilliant war, won the Military Cross, was Mentioned in Despatches and was severely wounded. He survived the war, having been promoted to captain in the newly formed Royal Air Force. In 1919 he was posted to Royal Air Force, Andover, from whence he often visited his old school. Late in 1919 he was infected with dysentery. His constitution was so impaired by the severity of his war wounds that he was unable to beat off the disease. He died on 20 November 1919, a late victim of the war.

W.M. Cooper, whose bowling was singled out for praise, became captain of school in 1915. He took the entrance examination for the Royal

Military College, Sandhurst, in February 1916 and came second on the list, gaining a Prize Cadetship. After training, he was commissioned as a second lieutenant in the 2nd Battalion, The Royal Worcester Regiment, and was killed in action on Sunday 17 February 1917 aged nineteeen. He was one of four captains of his school to be killed in the war.

R.C. Bardsley, who was out through playing back when he ought to have played forward, left school in 1914 to volunteer for the 4th Battalion, Royal Berkshire Regiment and, clearly a good soldier, was a lance corporal by December of that year. By April 1916 he was commissioned second lieutenant in the Manchester Regiment and had attained the rank of captain by 8 October 1917, when he was severely wounded in the right arm.

W.L. Pauer, who also played a blind swipe and paid the natural penalty, became captain of school in 1915. By April of that year he was a cadet at the Royal Military College, Sandhurst. By December 1915 he was a second lieutenant in the Devonshire Regiment. He was severely wounded in July 1916. After this, things changed for W.L. Pauer. He appears to have resigned or lost his commission and next emerges as a corporal in the Munster Fusiliers. Did he go to Ireland to volunteer as a private soldier, no questions asked? His school magazine, usually ready to record the events in the life of captains of school, remained strangely silent on the matter. He became a sniper and by July 1918 was wounded a second time and awarded both the Military Medal and the *Médaille Militaire*. During the retreat in March 1918, in the face of the massive German attack known as Operation Michael, he was awarded a bar to his Military Medal and made a king's sergeant on the field. He must have fought brilliantly for, in December 1918, King's Sergeant W.L. Pauer was awarded the Distinguished Conduct Medal.

During Operation Michael, a total of sixty-three German divisions had attacked over a sixty-mile front, overwhelming the French and British, and advancing almost to within fifty miles of Paris. The Germans took around 60,000 prisoners, inflicted 164,000 casualties on the British and 70,000 on the French and they themselves suffered 160,000 casualties and lost 70,000 as POWs.

B.H. Churchill, who 'kept wicket excellently', attended the Royal Military College, Sandhurst, was commissioned second lieutenant in the Royal Field Artillery and was awarded the Military Cross and the *Croix de Guerre* in 1918. The Royal Field Artillery had come into existence on 1 July 1899, when it was formed from part of the Royal Artillery. During the First World War it was equipped with medium-calibre guns and howitzers and it was deployed close to the front line. In 1924 it was amalgamated once again with the Royal Artillery.

There were, of course, four other schoolboys in the XI, three of whom were commissioned in the army. L.C. Ambrose served as a second lieutenant in the Somerset Light Infantry, J.H.D. Faithfull as a second lieutenant in the Army Service Corps and A.S. Higlett, who was wounded, as a second lieutenant in the Royal Field Artillery. Of T.N. Middleton, there is no trace in the records.

In all, of the team that played against the MCC on 18 June 1914, one was killed in action, six were wounded – one of whom died after the war – and one was taken prisoner. They accumulated two Military Crosses, two Military Medals, one Distinguished Service Medal, one Mention in Despatches, one *Croix de Guerre* and one *Médaille Militaire*. That was not all, of course. Of the 1914 Rugby XV, many of whom were to see action within a year of leaving school, five lost their lives and two were wounded. Of the 1911 Rugby XV, seven members lost their lives and others were wounded. They were the sacrificial warriors, whom the public school system had done so much to create. In the book *Old School Ties – Educating for Empire and War*, Martin Parsons and the present author wrote that 'the death toll amongst the young men from public schools in the Great War was disproportionately high.' Reading School recorded that 500 former pupils served their country. Forty-three received gallantry awards and eighty-five lost their lives. Of the eighty-five to die, one was seventeen, two were eighteen and nine were nineteen. Perhaps the most telling statistic of them all is that twenty-six of the eighty-five killed were second lieutenants. The lower age limit at which young men could volunteer for commissioned service was seventeen, as compared to nineteen for private soldiers.

Compared to other ranks, the rate at which second lieutenants in infantry regiments were killed was disproportionate. This high casualty rate among junior officers was caused by a number of factors. This was the last war in which young subalterns led disciplined charges in parade formation from the front, whilst wearing distinctive uniforms and Sam Browns. Their weapon was the pistol and they sometimes, at least before Loos, brandished their swords. There were some notable cases when rugby footballs were kicked ahead of the charge and it was not unknown for some young squire to sound his hunting horn for encouragement. It is not just for egalitarian purposes that officers and NCOs of the modern British Army wear the same battle fatigues as their men and have their rank badges displayed inconspicuously on their chests, rather than on their shoulders. Leaders are crucial in war. Snipers and marksmen knew this and acted upon it with clinical efficiency, and still do.

Some of these gallant young men wrote letters to the editor of the *Reading School Magazine*. In August 1914, when Kitchener famously called for volunteers for his New Army, John William Victor Blazey was a seventeen-year-old clerk in the continental office of Messrs Huntley and Palmers, the biscuit manufacturers in Reading. Along with thousands of British boys at the time, he lied about his age and took the King's shilling. In July 1915, by then a private soldier in France with the 1st Battalion, the Royal Berkshire Regiment, he wrote this:

I thought you might like to have a line telling you a few experiences to date of trench warfare and life in general out here. First of all I do not wish to convey the impression which one would gather from reading the Reading local papers, i.e., that we have been in action, but we have had several sufficiently exciting and nerve-racking days for most people's liking. So far it has generally been on Sunday that we have been particularly 'favoured' with shell-fire and it is from these bombardments that our few casualties, for the most part, have occurred.

Although we are in quite an advanced part of the line, it is at present comparatively quiet, the object being, I think, to push up our immediate flanks until they are on a level with us. This policy is succeeding if the reports we hear are true, but the process is of necessity very slow.

Our life consists of four days in the trenches, followed by four days in support about a mile behind the firing line, and this second period is taken up with nearly unending fatigues, such as taking rations up to the half battalion doing duty in the trenches, digging fresh trenches, and above all making ourselves generally useful.

The two first-mentioned jobs are quite dangerous as, if not more so, than being 'in' as we call it, for the Germans have machine guns trained on all roads leading trench wards, and at frequent intervals 'let rip' in the hope of catching one of our parties. There are hundreds of stray bullets flying about too and every now and then someone gets one, and if the wound is not too serious, is talked about as being a 'lucky devil', and other things, for it means a holiday in England. But the spirits of all concerned out here are tip-top, and although few venture opinions as to the duration of the war, optimism reigns supreme. And that, to my mind, is a great factor in our favour.

I'm afraid I'm now the only Old Redingensian left in the Battalion.

I've every reason to believe that my application for a Commission would have materialised some time ago had I let it continue, but seven months training in England was so wearying that I jumped at the idea of coming out here and cancelled the application. And I must say I don't regret it in the least, for on the whole one couldn't wish to run across a better lot of fellows.

It was with deep regret that I heard of the death in action of Lieutenants Hawkins and Giles Ayres, also Captain Belcher; but it is certain that each one died as an Englishman should, and no greater tribute could be paid to anyone. Likewise I was glad to hear that Wells and Baseden are progressing favourably; of course it is inevitable that the old School should suffer some losses, but they may be as light as possible is the only hope.

To turn to a lighter subject. I hope that the XI will do really well again this season, young though the talent may be! It is a noticeable fact that all the casualties connected with the School, so far as I know, have happened to those who were to the front in sport, and every branch of athletics will be hard hit before this war is over, I fear.

Please give my kind regards to all those masters whom I knew and tell Mr. Crook that my OTC training served me in good stead.

It is a letter which is redolent of the attitudes widely held at the time in which it was written and they are analysed in detail elsewhere. It is, for the moment, enough to learn of John's sad fate and that of the friends he mentions in his letter. We are able to do so because of a remarkable collection of letters made available by the principal of Reading School. In the December 1915 *Reading School Magazine*, the following notice appeared:

Information has been received by his parents, who reside at 34, Bulmershe Rd. Reading, that their son, 2nd Lieutenant J.W. Blazey, was killed in action on September 28th, aged 18. Lieutenant Blazey was an old boy of Reading School and was a member of the Officers' Training Corps;

he won colours in Cricket and was a member of the Rugby XV. He was engaged in the Continental Office of Messrs. Huntley and Palmers. He joined the Army as a private early in August 1914, and after going to the Front in March he returned home last August and received a commission. Information shows that his company was ordered to attack in the recent advance. The assault was met by a strong force. 2nd Lieutenant Haigh, 69 Hamilton Rd. Reading, who was wounded, says that he saw Lieut. Blazey and a little band of men, surrounded by superior numbers of Germans and that there was little hope of them escaping alive.

John Blazey's recruitment into the army as a seventeen-year-old boy and his death at the age of eighteen was accepted as nothing unusual. His letter from the trenches becomes even more remarkable when we learn the fate of those friends he mentions. So, what happened to Lieutenants Hawkins and Giles Ayres and Captain Belcher?

Captain Belcher was an assistant master at Brighton College, then at Reading School where he may have taught John Blazey. He was a lieutenant in the OTC and on the seconded list at the outbreak of war. He joined the 3rd Battalion, Royal Berkshire Regiment, with which he saw fierce fighting in the autumn of 1914. He was Mentioned in Despatches in January 1915 and was awarded the Military Cross. He was promoted to captain and was killed in action on Saturday 15 May 1915 while attached to the 1st Berkshire Regiment.

Second Lieutenant Oliver Luther Hawkins, 3rd Battalion, East Yorkshire Regiment, died of wounds near Ypres on 26 April 1915. He was for several years captain of Reading School and would, for that reason alone, have been admired by John Blazey. On leaving school he studied at Marberg University before going into residence at Jesus College, Cambridge.

Lieutenant Giles Fredrick Ayres, 3rd Battalion, Lincolnshire Regiment (to which he was attached from the Dorset Regiment), was shot through the heart leading a charge on 9 May 1915. He wrote a poignant letter home on 8 May 1915, as he was mentally preparing himself to lead his men 'over the parapet' the following day. He was an old boy of Reading School and a leader of the Old Boys' Sports Club. It is a privilege to publish the following extracts from his letter, in which he conveyed in simple words the powerful ideology that prevailed among many young soldiers at the time:

Just a line to tell you the day has arrived. Tomorrow we go into our position, and there is to be a tremendous attack. You will read about it in the papers. Oh! may it be a success. Of course I ought not to write about this, but it matters not; it will either be good or bad by the time you receive this letter and I expect that I shall be on the way home wounded or shall remain here for ever ... the first I hope. I do so want to see you all again. I am going over the parapet with a shout of 'School' on my lips and then pray God's will be done!

I am writing in a little out-house where I am sleeping on straw tonight. Please do not send another parcel until you receive a postcard from me to let you know the result. I do not know what else to write about, except to say several fellow officers in the Dorsets have been wounded or killed. Well I must close, I have heaps to do, and must try to sleep tonight. If the worst comes to the worst, tell any young fellows in Reading who can, and there are many, that they must come and take our places.

If that was the end of the matter, it would be enough, but what of John Blazey's two friends, Wells and Baseden?

Lieutenant Eric Baseden, Royal Berkshire Regiment, was killed in action on Thursday 26 October 1916, whilst gallantly leading a platoon. A Lieutenant Mackinlay of the signal company wrote this to Eric's parents in December 1916:

Although I have only known your son for six months or so, we saw a good deal of each other and had become great friends. He was attached to this company until recently, and worked with me for several months preparing for the 1st July. I count it a great privilege to have regarded him as one of my friends. He was always so cheery and bright in difficult times, and took his hardships and disappointments like a man. If he had not been such a good fellow he would have been seconded to Signals some time ago. We all tried hard to get his papers through, but the battalion, knowing what they would lose if they lost him, refused to sanction, and he returned to lay down his life as cheerily as one would expect who knew him.

I know what disappointment the refusal of a transfer was to him, but I admired him even more than before, if that were possible, for the way he took it. His battalion went over the parapet two days after I saw him last and he came through safely. Then his battalion were

[sic] withdrawn to support trenches a few yards back. Eric was killed instantaneously by a shell while in the trenches, and was buried by his men immediately behind the trench. I find it hard to realise he has gone. I sympathise most deeply with you. You have lost a son and I have lost a very dear friend.

And Wells? He was educated at Kendrick Boys' School, which was amalgamated with Reading School in 1914. He went off to adventure in Canada after leaving school and took a job helping to construct a railway through the wild country north of Ontario. He enlisted in the Canadian Army on the first day of the war. On 14 March 1915, Private D.H. Wells of the Canadian Contingent wrote the following:

It is a Sunday evening, a mild spring night, and there is a fearful bombardment going on. For a couple of hours there has been a regular storm of thunder from hundreds of guns and there must be a terrible scrap going on somewhere.

There is an air of hope and expectancy about, you can feel and see it everywhere. We know that we are top dogs now but it is a question of a week or two. There are going to be heavy casualty lists, but it is the price of advance, and it is a damned sight better to go down advancing than retreating.

I got a pass out yesterday and went down town for a shave and a good feed. An English band was playing in the Square and the enthusiasm was great when the 'Marseilles' was played. As we listened, round the corner came an endless stream of Paris motor-buses, and then transports of all sorts. There were dispatch riders tearing through, Staff Officers strolling around, cavalry trotting through in twos and threes, ambulance wagons, London general omnibuses, and so on in spite of the music you knew it was WAR, WAR, WAR, everywhere about.

I wish you could have been in the square for a few minutes, and have seen the little groups of French soldiers, and their blue serge and red pants, in strange contrast to our dull khaki; or groups of civilians excitedly discussing the latest news and commenting on the future; or the little boys in their 'kepis' and cloaks, eyeing you as though you were a fresh animal at the Zoo.

Last night a brigade of cavalry passed through in a seemingly endless stream, smoking and whistling as though nothing much was wrong, and yet they had been through the whole weary seven months of it and been through hell in that time.

Bye the bye, it's going to be a great time for the cavalry soon and they won't have to go into the trenches much longer.

I was talking to a fellow in the [censored] who has been through everything. I was speaking about the reports in the papers of men simply longing to get back to the war, and expressed my doubts as to the sincerity of these reports; and he said: 'There are 25 left out of my regiment and I got five days leave some time ago and if I thought I was going back to the trenches I should never have gone back'.

D.H. Wells was a remarkable man. He was wounded at Ypres in May 1915 and afterwards gained a commission as a second lieutenant in the Yorkshire and Lancashire Regiment. He was awarded a Military Cross for conspicuous gallantry and devotion to duty when in command of a patrol. He was killed in action on 3 May 1917. A friend wrote this to his parents:

Amongst the officers and men in this battalion, especially the latter, he was worshipped, and it is by a man's followers that you can judge him best. His death has been deeply felt from the Colonel downwards. Our objective was resisted strongly, and so after a first and hopeless attempt we withdrew and had another attempt. 'Duggie' was wounded in the first, but would not leave his men, he was again wounded in the second attempt and reached the trench with only five men, but undaunted he led a bombing attack with his few and was killed attempting to capture a German machine gun at hopeless odds. He has again been recommended, which goes to prove that he was undoubtedly one of the best soldiers in the battalion, certainly quite the best friend one could wish for.

These stories and letters are not unusual. Their like can be found with a minimum of diligence in the archives of most public schools in England. They show no signs of bitterness but plenty of enthusiasm and, to our ears, astonishing loyalty to their old school. The bitterness which pervades much of the postwar literature may have appeared later when the survivors had time to reflect but, since so many old boys visited their school during and after the war, some sign of disillusionment might have been expected. Perhaps it was censored for there is none in the school magazine.

There is clear evidence that stories such as that of Captain F.L.M. Shirley RAF, he who captained the school cricket team in 1914, formed the basis of the yarns aimed at boys, *Winning his Wings: a Story of the RAF*, the first of a number of very successful flying stories to be written by Percy F. Westerman in 1919. Whatever others may assert, based on the writings of some of the war poets, what we see in the Reading School collection of letters is the emergence of the authentic sacrificial schoolboy who was capable, in the face of almost certain death, of leading his men over the top with the shout of 'School' on his lips and a prayer in his heart. The system which produced him, and hurled him willingly into withering machine-gun fire, must have been very powerful indeed. To his parents and his relatives, it must have been difficult to stomach the growing postwar notion that he and his kind died a futile death.

If we are to understand why these boys were capable of such heroic leadership, we need to study their indoctrination at school with care. Reading School will serve as a useful case study. It had the full gamut of management systems in place, which are recognised by historians as common at that time. A number of public schools were founded in the decade of the 1870s. They were given a fillip by a significant change in entrance requirements to the public services which had hitherto been somewhat skewed in the hereditary direction. The Indian Civil Service was first recruited from successful candidates in an examination in 1855 and the Home Civil Service followed suit in its recruiting in 1870. Gladstone was strong enough to challenge the last bastion of privilege when he abolished the purchase of officers' commissions in the army in 1871. It became the aim of the new public schools to get candidates into the military academies at Sandhurst and Woolwich by examination, and they set up army classes for this purpose.

Reading School was unusual amongst the aspirant Victorian public schools, since it had reinvented itself in the latter part of the nineteenth century. At just about the time other schools were developing a tradition, Reading School could already boast a long and illustrious history in its prospectus. The school had been re-founded in 1486 and there is strong evidence that it was in existence in 1125.

There were a number of eminent alumni and care was taken to advertise the names of those deceased on memorial tablets in the main school and the school chapel. The military and imperialist tendencies are amply illustrated by the following three heroes whose names appear in prominent positions: Henry Vansittart, friend of Clive of India, was governor of Bengal from 1759 to 1764; Lieutenant-General Sir John Keen was created Baron Keen of Guznee (Ghaznī) for his efforts in the First Afghan War; and the heroic Captain Hastings Harrington, of the Bengal Artillery, was awarded a Victoria Cross for his part in the relief of the garrison of Lucknow during the Indian Mutiny.

The headmasters of public schools were often Oxbridge-educated ordained priests of the Church of England. A doctorate of divinity was almost de rigueur, as was an enthusiasm for competitive sport, the British Empire and the monarchy. The cliché, which sums up their philosophy well enough, is militant muscular Christianity.

It is almost impossible to escape the suggestion that Dr William Charles Eppstein, headmaster of Reading School from 1894 to 1914, embodies the stereotype just a little too well. His father was John Moses Eppstein, who was born in Russia in 1827 and who became a naturalised British subject, an Anglican priest and a missionary, serving in Iraq and Turkey. William, his eldest child, was born in Baghdad in 1864 and was educated at the British Commercial School in Smyrna and Lord Williams School, Thame, Oxfordshire. He gained a BA at St John's College, Oxford, and accepted his MA in 1889. He was ordained deacon in London in 1887 and became a priest in 1888. He served as curate of St Mary's, Spital Square, and later in Stowmarket, Suffolk. His teaching career commenced in 1891 and he was appointed headmaster of Reading School in 1894. He achieved the final accolade of a doctorate of divinity in 1905. He left the school in some financial difficulty in 1914, having run it as a personal fief through his own bank account.

The school was bailed out by an amalgamation with Kendrick Boys' School, a commercial rather than a public school, a new headmaster and a prudent bursar. This amalgamation brought boys of the aspirational lower middle class into the school, with consequences for us and our boy soldiers.[2]

Eppstein's educational aims were interesting and are best illustrated by the successes he chose to emphasise in 1905, when he had been headmaster for more than eleven years. Eighteen boys had won open scholarships to Oxford or Cambridge. Six boys had gained admission to the RMC, Sandhurst, and three had gained admission to the RMC, Woolwich. Three had passed the examination for the Indian Police and eight had passed the examination for HMS *Britannia*. Two had obtained Eastern cadetships and one a student interpretership. Eppstein was in the business of training imperial leaders and, inadvertently, sacrificial schoolboys for the war to come.

The tools Eppstein used to achieve his aims were common to most similar institutions, these being a staff made up of Oxford and Cambridge men; the school chapel; the prefectorial system; the cadet corps; the honours boards prominently displayed around the school; the house system which satisfied the inherent need of adolescent boys for fierce competition and peer grouping; the games field which absorbed youthful motor energies; and the school magazine, which became his propaganda arm. All these forces combined to harness and direct male adolescent aggression. They also emphasised the leadership qualities, teamwork principles and discipline, which are essential in responding to natural disasters and overcoming difficulties in dangerous circumstances, especially in battle. It was invaluable to Kitchener's New Army and was one of the factors which enabled the British to produce a huge army from scratch, as it produced a group of young men who were trained in leadership and nurture. It is worth comparing it to the German day-gymnasium system. This emphasised academic hothousing and very strict discipline but lacked the peer group support that was the central pillar of the British public school.[3]

The prefectorial system, said to have been instituted by Arnold at Rugby, was a selective system into which boys, even from scholarship or freeplacer backgrounds, were admitted to a ruling elite, given responsibilities and accorded special privileges. They adopted titles such as house captain or school captain and filled specific executive roles. They often wore subtle modifications of school uniform, as an indication of their status, and had their own common room to reinforce their power and insularity from the rest of the school. They could punish their juniors, sometimes being able to use the cane, and prescribe tasks or extra drills. They acted as leaders, heroes, guides and mentors for their juniors. The effect of the system reached right down to the lower school and helped shape the behaviour of the great majority who aspired to succeed to its ranks. It was a powerful system of control, with a dual purpose. It allowed each school to promote its aims by selecting from its ranks those pupils who epitomised its ideals and, in return, gave training in the art of leadership. In boarding schools during term time, prefects were never off duty. They learnt to live with responsibility, even when they were asleep.

Many schools had formed cadet corps as a result of the provision in the Volunteers Act of 1863 which enabled them to do so. Charterhouse and Dulwich founded theirs in 1870 and, in the late 1880s and 1890s, the cadet movement spread into working-class districts of cities, especially the East End of London. For example, a Toynbee Hall cadet corps was formed in 1886, followed by others in Tower Hamlets and Southwark.[4]

The cadet corps at Reading School was formed at the height of the Boer War in May 1900, the month Mafeking was relieved. It was affiliated to the 1st London Royal Engineer Volunteers. Much of its history between 1901 and 1908 was, therefore, closely associated with the Volunteer movement. One of the housemasters, A.W. Gundry, was appointed captain of the corps and two senior boys were appointed second lieutenants to assist him. Some members of the teaching staff joined the ranks to give encouragement to the boys. Captain Gundry was a typical public school housemaster of this period, being a sometime scholar of Emmanuel College, Cambridge. He had been first in the Second Class of the Classical Tripos and first in the Ceylon Civil Service examination, though whether or not he served in Ceylon is unclear. He was an enthusiastic Volunteer and a fine fencer.

In 1900 the 1st London Royal Engineer Volunteers was a battalion of over 800 strong, commanded by Colonel Wood. He seconded one of his officers, Captain Dance RE, to the school as adjutant of the corps. Captain Dance was said to have had experience in the Sudan. A qualified sergeant instructor, Sergeant Eynott, late of the Royal Engineers, was appointed by the school. His salary was to be in the region of £104 per annum, of which £25 appears to have been contributed by the headmaster from his own private income. In 1901 Sergeant Eynott was recalled to active service in South Africa and he was replaced by Quartermaster Sergeant C. Taylor.

The question of uniform for the boys was the subject of hot debate. Many in the Public School Cadet Corps were still wearing scarlet, blue or green. It was not until 1901 that it was decided that the regular army was to wear khaki in times of peace as well as in war. At Reading the matter was settled in favour of khaki and the early photographs of the corps are, therefore, unique and interesting to students of military uniforms of the period. An armoury was built and thirty Lee-Metford rifles were supplied, half of which were serviceable weapons capable of live firing and half for drill purposes. A range was constructed in the school grounds for small-bore shooting and a shooting VII was trained on the local Volunteer ranges to compete at the Open Public School Shoot at Bisley.

A cyclist section was raised and it appeared occasionally as a form of cavalry on field days. A band was formed in 1903, at first a drum and fife band for younger cadets, who found it hard to carry rifles on field days. A bugle corps was later added.

The Reading School Corps attended the Public School Field Days on the training areas around Aldershot. These were massive affairs when hundreds of cadets from numerous schools in the area converged for a set-piece mock battle commanded by a regular army officer. Each summer the Reading Corps joined its 800-strong parent unit, the 1st London REV, at camp. These were always on greenfield sites at Arundel or Littlehampton.

Volunteer Reviews were great public spectacles. On 29 June 1901, the 1st London REV held theirs in Regents Park and the Reading School Corps attended. According to an eyewitness account, the park was lined with crowds of spectators. On the largest stretch of grass, a long line of men, wearing scarlet coats and dark trousers with broad stripes, was lined up. On the left of the line were two neat companies of Reading School cadets in khaki. Marching with the khaki warriors were three very small boys, too young to carry rifles but otherwise soldiers in miniature. One of them was very redheaded, and, with his crimson top and very thin little body, looked just like a fishing float. Behind were the band, signallers, stretcher bearers and some fully horsed ammunition carts.

In due course the inspecting officer arrived, riding his charger and dressed in his blues and cocked hat.''Ere comes the Dook of Wellington' shouted a small onlooker, as the colonel's horse tittuped across the grass. With the battalion in open order, he commenced to ride slowly through the lines, his horse dancing a little to indicate pride. Then followed battalion drill, culminating in the march past in quarter column. At the conclusion of the march past, the order 'change ranks' brought the Reading School Corps to the head of the column, which it led off in the return march to the strains of the British Grenadiers. More movements followed and, at 8 o'clock, the boys in khaki moved off homeward to the cheers of their new friends.

On 15 September 1908 the long affiliation with the Volunteer movement came to an end for Reading School, as a result of changes made by the secretary of state for war, Richard Haldane. By 1907 Haldane had completed his radical reforms of the regular army and had turned his attention to the auxiliary forces, the Militia, the Yeomanry and the Volunteers, which he amalgamated to form the Territorial Force. The financial burden was removed from the commanding officers of the volunteer units and transferred to county Territorial Associations, which were now responsible for the recruitment and administration of the Territorial Forces in their county.

The establishment of Officer Training Corps at public schools and universities was included in this reorganisation. Haldane argued that, to provide leadership for an expanded army in times of national emergency, the Officer Corps would have to expand rapidly. The Officer Training Corps were specifically formed to train young middle-class men for military leadership. The instrument of this training was the course of instruction laid down by the Army Council, leading up to the examination for Certificate A.

To gain a Certificate A, a cadet would be examined in tactics, training a company in the field, knowledge of the army, methods of recon-naissance and the general outlines of a battle. He would be required to demonstrate his ability to drill bodies of troops and understand the rifle and the theory of rifle fire. The possession of a Certificate A would qualify the holder, other things being equal, for the rank of lieutenant in the new Territorial Force, or procure for him the advantage of 200 marks if he was accepted into Woolwich or Sandhurst. A school corps could claim a grant of £10 for each cadet who gained both a Certificate A and was accepted for a commission in the Territorial Force. In Reading School the training for the certificate took three years. The headmaster at the time complained that the work required of OTCs by the War Office had required other schools to employ regular officers to assist their corps.

When Reading School Corps was founded in 1900, there were 150 pupils on the school roll, of whom sixty or so were boarders. By the end of the war in 1918, there were 358 boys in the school. On 14 December 1918, the school magazine was reporting that 418 past pupils of the school had served in all branches of the armed forces and that 77 of them had been killed in action or had died as a result of wounds received.

In fact, the number of war dead was later amended to 82. A casualty rate of almost twenty per cent was a high price to pay for boys of this generation, for that is all many of them were. It is remarkable that so many were prepared not only to lay down their lives for their beliefs but also to exhort other members of the school, not yet nineteen, to take their places should they fall in battle. The number of decorations and gallantry awards won by Reading School old boys is creditable, being, at least, seven DSOs, twenty-eight MCs (three with Bar), one DSM, one DCM, one MM and Bar, twelve Mentions in Despatches, at least two *Légions d'honneur* and two *Médailles Militaire*.

The prefectorial system and the OTC were not the only weapons at the disposal of the good Dr Eppstein. He made sure that the Old Boys' Club met regularly and he supported the founding of an old boys' Masonic lodge in 1911. He personally encouraged competitive sport, himself playing football and cricket for his school in the early days. He was said to have been a fine left-arm bowler and to have used the same arm to flog those of his pupils who needed extra motivation.

He was a born publicist and used the school magazine to convey a clear, consistent message to his pupils and their parents. The magazine, like so many others, became the 'unremitting [agent] of seduction for an imperial dream of noble service and intoxicating adventure.'[5] By publishing letters from old boys in the far-flung Empire, he inculcated a sense of imperial duty and English superiority and certainty. His magazine was a recruiting organ for the army, a travel magazine and a prospectus for the colonies. It was the certainty and sense of duty conveyed through his magazine, his sermons in chapel and his public speeches, which motivated his pupils to volunteer for service in the First World War and to act with courage as young leaders in the face of incredible odds.

Letters from young patriots engaged in some imperial venture or other were published frequently as an inspiration to others. Two extracts will suffice to illustrate the point. Philip Percival wrote the first letter from his farm in Limoru, British East Africa, in 1910. He was to become famous as Ernest Hemingway's white hunter during the great writer's safari in 1933. Hemingway fictionalised the safari in his small book *The Green Hills of Africa*, in which he called Percival 'Pop' or 'Jackson Phillips'. Hemingway's short story *The Snows of Kilimanjaro* is an elaboration of one of Percival's own fireside tales, with which he charmed and educated Hemingway while they were in camp. The source of some other campfire yarns, which appeared in *The Green Hills of Africa*, can be discerned in this letter:

> You asked about life out here, so here goes for a few of my hunting experiences … I killed my first lion easily; at the time I was ostrich catching with a friend, he and I being the first to try ostrich farming in British East Africa … I remember another time I was out by myself riding round when I came upon three lions, two fine-maned lions and a very bad tempered lioness. I was off my pony (who had not seen or winded them), and was trying to see something definite to shoot at (they were all lying asleep in a heap), when one looked up and seeing me, gave a grunt and bolted: the second lion followed suit, but the lioness started walking slowly towards me growling and lashing her tail about. Jumping on my pony I was soon on terms with one of the runaways, who finding running useless, lay down and awaited developments. The fun began, my poor pony got the fidgets, wouldn't let me shoot off her back, went mad when I tried to shoot holding the reins over my arm, and was generally a nuisance. To make a long story short, I spent a very exciting two hours, was charged three times, and the last time I was in such a hurry to get on, and the pony in such a hurry to get away, that I abandoned my rifle and climbed on anyhow, fairly fled with the old lion growling behind me. Once I was on the way the lion lost no time in getting into the long grass, and I was able to go back and get my rifle …
>
> I never had serious trouble with rhino or elephant, in both cases 'wind' is the thing to watch. In the long grass rhino are rather beastly, as one often walks on to them unexpectedly, and they come snorting and blundering at one like a runaway engine, giving one quite a start to say the least of it. Fortunately, as a rule, they are easily turned by a shot at the nose.
>
> Quite recently I got scared by elephants. I had followed the spoor of a herd into the thick forest and came on them all scattered out feeding; a mob of about twenty-five cows and calves got my wind and came to investigate, making the most appalling noise as they crashed along. I was devotedly thankful when I was well out of it.

Another example is a letter from Captain C.A.S. Lawrance DSO written in British Somaliland in 1906. Lawrance went on to become the governor general and commander-in-chief of British Somaliland and was awarded both the KBE and the KCMG:

I have just returned after twenty-four hours hard going after a lion; we were hot on its tracks most of the time, but lost them and had to return here: now he has followed us up and is quite near us in the jungle. I heard a lion early this morning and hope to get another go at him, but think I shall wait until I know of a kill; this ground is so hard that tracking is very difficult.

Am having a grand time most days trying to make four camels draw a nine-pound gun about; having only home-made rope harness, and the animals have never done anything like this before, we have some exciting times. A few days ago the gun ran away, nearly killing the wretched camels and a dozen Somalis, and finished taking a piece out of the fort wall.

About two weeks ago I helped dig up the remains of two officers who had been buried about two years ago; we have to send them to Berbera to be reburied in the cemetery there, since we may be leaving this part of the country altogether, and some of the Somalis are not good to English graves.

We had a village on fire a night or two ago; it was great burn since all the huts are made of wood and grass. Of course the Somalis, at a time like this, are quite helpless, and were quite content to let the whole thing burn down. After some time we got it under control by cutting a passage through the huts and throwing sand on the flame – there was no water to spare for fires …

Henty and the prolific *Boys' Own* adventure story writers would strive to fictionalise these heroics and would find a ready market among all classes.[6]

OUTSTANDING DEBTS OF COURAGE

And clink of shovels deepened the shallow trench.
The place was rotten with dead; green clumsy legs
High booted, sprawled and grovelled along the saps
And trunks, faced downward, in the sucking mud,
Wallowed like trodden sand bags loosely filled;
And naked sodden buttocks, mats of hair,
Bulged, clotted heads slept in the plastering slime.

Siegfried Sassoon.

Those who risk their lives for a cause are admired by those who hold that the cause is just. Since the First World War a number of people have concluded that the enormous loss of life was futile. It does not help that so many of the dead have no known grave. The terrible experiences of trench warfare must have been hard enough to endure. To leave the relative security of the trench and charge the enemy must have required extraordinary motivation. Some soldiers were animated by personal ambition, some by regimental tradition and not a few by the fear of being shot for cowardice.

Ambition allied to talent can be formidable. In 1877 Will Robertson, aged seventeen, was a footman in the service of the Cardigan family at Deene Park, Northamptonshire. The 7th Earl of Cardigan had, of course, misheard Lord Raglan's orders at Balaclava and initiated the Charge of the Light Brigade. No doubt there were sufficient mementoes of a military nature in the big house at Deene Park to impress the below-stairs staff, for Will Robertson, after four years in domestic service, was inspired to join the army. Much later in life, after an adventurous and well-rewarded career, Will wrote:

> I was seventeen and three-quarters years old when I took the Queen's Shilling from a recruiting sergeant in the city of Worcester on the 13th November 1877. The minimum age for enlistment was eighteen, but as I was tall for my years the sergeant said that the deficient three months would involve no difficulty, and he promptly wrote me down as eighteen years and three months, so as to be on the safe side.

Will was the son of Thomas Robertson, who ran a combined village post office and tailoring business at Welbourn in Lincolnshire. Will's mother, Ann Dexter Robertson, was in no doubt that all soldiers were ignorant, drunken and licentious. She was deeply upset that her son should have enlisted and wrote to him in some distress:

> you never could mean what you put in your Letter on Sunday ... what cause have you for such a Low life ... you have as good a home as any one else in your station ... you know you are the Great Hope of the Family ... the Army is the refuge of all idle people ... I would rather Bury you than see you in a red coat.

Will was not deterred and joined 'G' Troop, 16th Lancers, at Aldershot. He spent ten and a half years in the ranks. He was a fine soldier and was promoted quickly. In March 1885 he was troop sergeant major and it was time to think about his career. He might have waited, as was expected, for the regimental sergeant major to retire or, as was most unusual, apply for a commission.

It took an NCO of enormous determination to apply for a commission in 1885, when the British Army was still in the thrall of a rigid and well-defended class structure. Commissioned rankers did not often survive the acute and detailed scrutiny of their accents and manners by the subalterns in the mess. Nor could ex-rankers survive the crippling financial burden, a legacy of the system whereby officers bought their commissions and their promotions. Though this system had been abolished in 1871, a private income was still indispensable for an officer. A cavalry officer needed, at the very least, £300 over and above his pay to compete on an equal footing in the social, sporting and sartorial competition of mess life. Officers in fashionable regiments got rid of social misfits with callous efficiency.

Will Robertson's best chance was to apply for a commission in India. Here he would be paid more and his expenses would be lower. He had managed to pass the necessary First Class Certificate in Education in 1883 but it was not until June 1888 that he was gazetted second lieutenant in the 3rd Dragoon Guards stationed at Muttra. There he was welcomed by his fellow officers despite the fact that, as he later wrote without rancour, water was the only drink he could afford when others were drinking champagne. He worked hard and saw plenty of action, notably on the Chitral Relief Column. This was commanded brilliantly by Fredrick Sleigh Roberts VC, who led an army of 10,000 men to the relief of Kandahar, covering a distance of over 300 miles in twenty-two days and defeating the Afghans.

Will, who was known as 'Wully', though not to his face, returned to Britain and joined the Staff College at Camberley in January 1897. He was the first ex-private soldier ever to do so. He was there at the right time, for among his contemporaries were Haig and Allenby. He was successful at Staff College and was posted to South Africa to join the staff of Colonel G.F.R. Henderson, the director of intelligence to Lord Roberts during the Boer War. From thence he was posted to the Intelligence Division at the War Office as a brevet lieutenant colonel in charge of the Foreign Section. It was during this time that he realised that Britain would have to fight Germany. He found himself back at Camberley in 1910 as commandant of the Staff College, where he was said to be very severe but at the same time human and encouraging.

The small British Expeditionary Force, under the less-than-secure leadership of Sir John French, found itself by 20 August 1914 on the left wing of the French Fifth Army, squarely in the path of the right wing of a ferocious German onslaught which had been launched through Belgium into France. Wully Robertson had been appointed quartermaster general of the BEF and had gone to France on 14 August to reconnoitre the ground. He anticipated that the BEF would soon be forced to retreat and laid his plans accordingly.[1]

The Germans had crossed into Belgium and eventually forced the surrender of Liège. The Belgian Army there had proved unexpectedly stubborn and had held up the German advance, resulting in some savage reprisals on the civilian population. Those regiments of the Belgian Army which did not surrender retreated to the west to join up with the BEF, then moved east to try to stop von Kluck's 1st Army in its tracks. The French were being pushed back in the south, suffering heavy losses, so the main thrust of the German attack was aimed directly, though inadvertently, at the BEF. Von Kluck's intelligence had been poor; the British Cavalry Division, under Allenby, had performed brilliantly and blinded his reconnaissance. Von Kluck had intended to outflank the heavily outnumbered men of the BEF but, instead, blundered straight into them.

By 22 August General Smith-Dorrien had moved II Corps of the BEF to Mons and had established a defensive line. At dawn the following day, the advance guard of the Germans arrived but was thwarted by the 4th Middlesex Regiment. Three hours later, eight German divisions arrived and attacked the northern end of the town. However, the 4th Middlesex was now accompanied by the 4th Royal Fusiliers. The Germans, advancing in close order, were easily repelled by the British who fired so rapidly that the Germans thought they were facing machine guns all along their front. Smith-Dorrien was quoted as saying:

> German losses were very heavy for they came on in dense formation, offering perfect targets, and it was not until they had been mowed down in thousands that they adopted more open formations.

The Battle of Mons, as it was to be called, was the first battle to be fought by the British against a European enemy since 1855, and the first fought by the British in Western Europe since 1815.[2] Despite the British success, when Smith-Dorrien heard that the Belgian Army was in retreat, he realised that he was in danger of being overwhelmed by superior numbers of Germans and was forced to order the retreat from Mons.

The British Army marched continuously for five days; men were so tired that many were hallucinating. This could account for the vision of the Angel of Mons, reported by troops. She was said to be wearing white and riding a white horse with a flaming sword in her hand and facing the German Army forbidding their progress. The troops set up a defensive line at Le Cateau on 25 August and were relieved by Haig's force which was fresh, having seen no action. On the 26th the situation once again became critical. Only the timely arrival of the French cavalry saved the day and kept the line together. The action at Le Cateau cost 7,800 casualties, out of the fighting force of 40,000. The British now withdrew to St Quentin. An attack by the Belgian Army slowed the Germans down, giving the BEF some breathing space. The Belgians and the French reserves managed to halt the German advance. The latter were so surprised at this that they turned their main thrust southwards. However, by the end of August 1914, the French, Belgian and British were in full retreat and Paris was threatened.[3] Throughout all this Wully Robertson had worked wonders as QMG. He wrote:

> In the retreat a large amount of clothing and equipment were either lost, captured or thrown away ... and it was my duty to see that it was immediately replaced ... the expedient was adopted of dumping supplies – flitches of bacon, sides of beef, cheese, boxes of biscuits, etc., alongside the road, so that the troops might help themselves as they passed.

The fall of Paris seemed imminent. Field Marshal Sir John French made plans to withdraw the BEF to the Channel ports, where they would be ready for immediate evacuation if necessary. In the meantime, the French military commander in Paris, General J.S. Gallieni, consulted the British secretary of state for war, Lord Kitchener, about the use of British forces to help him defend the city. Kitchener gave him overall command of the BEF and, in so doing, stopped Sir John French's planned withdrawal. Gallieni's plan was simple. All Allied units would counter-attack along the River Marne and stem the German advance. Reserve forces would be used to plug holes and attack the German flanks.

The Germans were in trouble. They had underestimated the number of troops needed for their grand plan and their extended supply lines led to serious logistical problems. This forced them to change their plans and attempt to swing east of Paris, rather than go round the capital to the west. What is more, Moltke, the German supreme commander, lost his nerve. In this regard the Germans were inflexible, and, without leadership, they began to flounder. The Battle of the Marne, in which the BEF played an important part, was won and Paris was saved. The Germans, having failed to win a quick victory, retreated seventy miles to the river Aisne. On 14 September German reserves arrived to stem their retreat and soon afterwards trench warfare set in all the way from the Channel coast in the north to the Alps in the south.

Now Wully Robertson had to worry about supplies. The British industrial system was unable to convert to a war footing quickly enough to supply the needs of the BEF in France and Robertson was forced by critical shortages to send constant requests to the War Office. He was particularly troubled by a lack of ammunition during the First Battle of Ypres when he was forced to ration the ammunition for field artillery, a factor which contributed to the heavy loss of life.

In January 1915 Robertson was invited to become chief of the General Staff of the BEF and in December 1915 he was brought home to become the chief of the Imperial General Staff, the first soldier to rise from the ranks to fill this supreme post. The recruiting sergeant in Worcester, who had pressed the King's shilling into the hand of the seventeen-year-old William Robertson, could not have imagined that he was responsible for enlisting the man who became Field Marshal Sir William Robert Robertson GCB, GCMG, GCVO, DSO, DCL, LLD.

Another superb regular army soldier, Private Edward Dwyer, was fighting with the 1st East Surrey Regiment during the retreat from Mons. On 30 May 1915 he wrote a letter to one of his officers, Lieutenant H.F. Stoneham, from a hospital ward. It is an important letter for a number of reasons. Firstly, it gives us a professional soldier's view of the retreat and its aftermath; secondly, he was a soldier in one of the army's most ancient and respected regiments and his letter is redolent of that unique spirit which was, and still is, the essence of the professional army; thirdly, he won the Victoria Cross for an act of supreme courage in a regimental action, which was an incomparable feat of arms; he was a boy of sixteen when he joined his regiment in 1911. It is a privilege to be able to include his letter verbatim. He was replying, with notable modesty, to a letter of congratulations on the award of his VC, which he had received from Stoneham:

Dear Sir,

Your kind and welcome letter of the 23 inst. has been forwarded to me. I was very surprised indeed to hear from you. Thank you sincerely, Sir, for the congratulations and I will endeavour to make myself worthy of them.

I sincerely hope you will soon be well again – your wound has taken a long time to heal. Sir, there are only a few of the old signallers left, Ede and Cooke. Collins, Hall, Gooch and Ellis. Sweeny, Lee and Smythe are at 14 Bde. Elson, Robbins, Newstead and Mobley are at home in Dover.

I quite well remember that day you were wounded, also Sgt's B. and R. Hunt were killed, that day Capt. Bowring was captured, and Capt. Hewitt was wounded, everything was in a pickle, Lt Colonel Longley being the coolest man.

I cannot really describe the events from the Marne to the Aisne, I was like one in a dream. About the beginning of October the [division] was booked for Antwerp but they were so hard pressed round La Bassee that we were stopped and sent there: an aeroplane raced our train and stopped us, and we went to relieve the French round La Bassee. The Regiment we took over from was the 14th Alpine Chasseurs and I have never seen such a sight. They left their trenches at 2'oclock in the afternoon and all the Germans did was to follow them up. The consequence was that they ran right into us and we left half our Division behind wounded. That was three weeks nightmare to me; they used to counter-attack every night and in the district could be seen the most awful cases of 'German Kultur', among the women and also the little girls of the age of thirteen. We lost Sgt. Faire and Cpl Cox round there.

The Indians relieved us there at the end of October and we roamed about a bit from one position to another until the middle of November when we went to Messines. Whilst there Col. Longley was taken from us and promoted Brig. Genl: then of the old officers all we have left was:– Mr. Roupell, Mr. Darwell, Capt White and Mr. Clarke, and the rest are all new.

Christmas was spent out of the trenches but we were in for the Old Year out and the New Year in. We were doing famously there, every man knew the ground off by heart, and in February they gradually started shifting us further up the line towards Ypres. From Messines we went to Kemmel and that was where Pte Smith – he was in your platoon – was killed. He was an Irishman and a good man too. Smith, Elmer and myself were always together. You remember Pte. Sadler, Sir, he was killed there and also Ackerman. All the time serving men were being picked off. If you joined the Regiment again, Sir, you would hardly know one man except Elmer. It is very miserable in the Regiment now all the old officers and men have gone.

Well, Sir, we went to Ypres, and well we knew it, but the worst was yet to come. After taking Hill 60 the Regiment went up there and shelled us with their 17 mm guns for three days and nights without a stop, but could not shift us. It was there that we lost Major Patterson – he was the CO. Poor Capt. W was blown to atoms, only a couple of pieces could be found of him, and Mr. Roupell still led 'A' Company until they were relieved, although he was three times wounded.

There we lost 15 officers including Capt. W. Mr. Clarke got a dose of gas but I believe he is alright, but, Sir, if any of Captain Wynyards's family inquire, don't tell them he was blown up.

I do not know who commands the Regiment now, but a Capt Oldham of the Norfolk Regiment had them but he is wounded now. I wish poor Elmer was here, Sir, he wrote to me and is so lonely on his own. He is Company Orderly. We used often sit and have a chat – Elmer, Vassey, Sadler, Mitchell and I, and they nearly always brought your name into the conversation with a few remembrances of the days of the Retirement.

I must really close, Sir, I have so many letters to write. Trusting you will excuse the scribble.

Your obedient servant,
Edward Dwyer L/C 10523

Apart from its value as an account of events during and immediately following the retreat from Mons, this letter demonstrates the important aspects of the British regimental system. Like the Royal Navy, some British regiments recruited young men and made special arrangements for training them. Colonel A.C. Ward OBE, president of the Queen's Royal Surrey Regiment Association, states that during the First World War the 'Queen's' raised thirty-one battalions and twenty-nine Young Soldiers' and Labour Units. Lance Corporal Edward Dwyer VC was a young soldier, recruited with care and trained by people who understood their trade. He proved to be intelligent and was chosen to be a signaller.

In the view of the Duke of Cambridge, grandson of George III and a cousin of Queen Victoria, who was colonel of the Hanoverian Guards at nine and major general at twenty-six, recruits must be caught young otherwise men settled down to some civil employment which promised them better wages and comfort than the army. He thought that, as a rule, those who enlisted after attaining the age of twenty were the failures of their callings. He also believed that the advantage of taking recruits young was that they were more easily trained than older men to habits of discipline. The disadvantage was that a half-grown lad was physically unable to support the hardships of war.

Edward Dwyer's letter, with its references to the young men with whom he had trained and lived, shows us his regiment acting as his family. From the colonel and the regimental sergeant major down to the new recruit, it represented home, profession and ideology. The officers' mess and the sergeants' mess would impose demands, which superseded the domestic imperatives of wives and children. Officers needed the permission of their colonel before they married and would rarely do so before they were twenty-five at least.

The regimental routine of training and sport, together with ceremonial and religious observance, would extend throughout the whole week and the whole year. There would be symbols of the regiment's history and associations, represented primarily by the regimental colours. The colours were the rallying point of the regiment in every sense. The silver and gold sculptures, which decorated the great dining tables in the messes, would embody the martial history as well as the patronage the regiment could command. For the new recruit, the ultimate ambition was to be the regimental sergeant major and the subaltern's aim was to command the regiment.

Throughout the whole of his life, each member of the regiment would see pictures of its adventures, its heroes, its battle honours and its peregrinations throughout the world. Officers and senior NCOs would be taught to display, to recognise, and to reward courage. That is why a good, well-led and well-trained regiment would be a formidable military unit, as was the 1st East Surrey Regiment in the defence of Hill 60, a commanding position overlooking the low ground towards Ypres.

For the 1st Battalion of the East Surrey Regiment, the three-day engagement on Hill 60 began on 19 April 1915, when they took over from the 13th Brigade which had captured it from the Germans on 17 April. The Germans were determined to retake the hill and launched a number of fierce attacks under heavy and continuous artillery bombardments.

At 3 p.m. on the 20th, the Germans assaulted the trench in which Pte Edward Dwyer was positioned. According to the regimental war diary, he 'distinguished himself by crawling up the parapet and flinging hand grenades at the enemy, he himself being under a perfect hail of enemy bombs.' For this act of courage, Edward Dwyer was awarded the Victoria Cross. His citation read:

> For conspicuous bravery and devotion to duty on Hill Sixty on 20th April 1915. When his trench was heavily attacked by German grenade throwers, he climbed on to the parapet and although subjected to a hail of bombs at close quarters, succeeded in dispersing the enemy by the effective use of hand grenades. Private Dwyer displayed great gallantry earlier in this day, in leaving his trench under heavy shell fire to bandage his wounded comrade.

It was a mark of extraordinary tenacity on display on Hill 60 that Edward Dwyer was only one of three members of the East Surrey Regiment who were awarded the VC for conspicuous gallantry. The others were Lieutenant G.R. Roupell and Second Lieutenant B.M. Geary. The Military Cross was awarded to Lieutenants T.H. Darwell and E.G.H. Clarke. Distinguished Conduct Medals were awarded to Sergeant Major A.J. Reid, Sergeants P. Griggs and W.E. Packard, Corporal W.H. Harding, Lance Corporal F.S. Martin and Privates A. Holtz and F. Grimwood. Nine members of the regiment were Mentioned in Despatches and three were awarded the Russian Cross of St George. Edward Dwyer recovered from his wounds and took some well-deserved leave in England, where he addressed recruiting meetings. He rejoined his battalion on 27 May 1916 at Arras and was killed in action at Leuze Wood four months later.[4]

Soldiers of the regular army and the volunteer new armies had been highly motivated on the whole. Conscription, when it came in 1916, brought many reluctant men into the service. After it was introduced, the problems of discipline changed in nature and required closer attention. Perhaps this contributed to an increase in executions for cowardice or desertion. For example, Private Thomas Hawkins was executed at 06:53 on 22 November 1917, having been tried for cowardice and desertion on more than one occasion while serving with the Royal West Surrey Regiment. He had enlisted on 8 September 1914, aged sixteen. In mitigation, at his field general court martial, Hawkins stated: 'I am

19 years and three months old. I enlisted at 16 years of age. I have been in France for 2 years and three months.'[5]

One of the shameful trends that emerged during the First World War was the reversion by the British Army to the execution of men convicted of desertion or cowardice. This is the more immoral because very young soldiers were among those shot. No British soldier had been executed between 1803 and the Boer War, when Kitchener confirmed the death sentence on the Australian Lieutenants Harry 'Breaker' Morant and Hancock who had been convicted of summarily executing twelve Boer prisoners. Morant appears to have acted in revenge for the killing of a friend, who was said to have been castrated and otherwise mutilated by Boers before he died. These executions were, and still remain, controversial. It resulted in the Australian government refusing to allow Australian soldiers convicted of capital crimes to be executed during the First World War. The tale of 'Breaker' Morant was made into a film in Australia in 1979. The film conveys the view that the courts martial were perfunctory and unfair.[6]

Even the best authorities differ as to how many British and Commonwealth soldiers were executed by firing squads during the war. The numbers given by Field Marshal Lord Carver in his book *Britain's Army in the 20th Century* are 245 for desertion and 37 for cowardice or similar offences. David Englander, in his essay 'Mutinies and Military Morale' in *The Oxford Illustrated History of the First World War*, states that the British carried out 346 executions. He also states that the French executed 700 and the Italians 750.[7] Stephen Stratford, in his online 'Study Room', gives a figure of 294 executed out of a total of 2,576 who were convicted of capital crimes. According to this source, the most lethal regiment to be in was probably the West Yorkshire Regiment, which convicted 44 and executed 12. Julian Putkowski, in his book *Shot at Dawn*, suggests that the number of British and Commonwealth soldiers executed for military offences in the war was 312.

Among these soldiers was James Crozier, a Belfast lad, who was shot at dawn for cowardice at the age of sixteen. He was dosed with rum until he was almost paralytic and dragged before the firing squad. There was a real fear amongst the officers supervising the execution that the firing squad would not obey the order to shoot. Private Abe Bevistein, also sixteen, was executed by a firing squad at Labourse, near Calais. He had been found guilty of deserting his post and had written:

We were in the trenches. I was so cold I went out. They took me to prison so I will have to go in front of the court. I will try my best to get out of it, so don't worry.

It is noted that four times more men deserted in Britain than in France and Belgium. For the record, Private George Stanley Peachment VC, 2nd Battalion, King's Royal Rifle Corps, went absent without leave for three days in England and was merely fined seven days' pay for his misdemeanour. He had enlisted at the age of seventeen years and eleven months but attested to being nineteen years and one month old on recruitment. Incidentally, he was probably older when he enlisted than many young officer volunteers, including John Kipling. However, George Peachment fought like a tiger. Here is part of the citation for his Victoria Cross:

> For most conspicuous bravery near Hulluch on 25th September 1915. During heavy fighting, when our front line was compelled to retire in order to reorganise, Private Peachment, seeing his Company Commander, Captain Dubs, lying wounded, crawled to assist him. The enemy's fire was intense, but, though there was a shell hole quite close in which a few men had taken cover, Private Peachment never thought of saving himself. He knelt in the open by his Commanding Officer and tried to help him, but while doing so was wounded by a bomb and a minute later was wounded by a bullet. He was one of the youngest men in his battalion when he gave this example of courage and self-sacrifice.

Captain Dubs survived the war and sent a letter to George's mother, in which he told her that her son 'lost his life trying to help me and no man can have been braver than he was.' Dubs went on to say: 'Your son died the finest death a man can die and he showed the greatest gallantry a man can show.' George's mother collected his VC from the King at Buckingham Palace on 29 November 1916 and it is now in the Ashcroft Collection. George's body was never recovered. He is commemorated on the Loos Memorial approximately 5km north-west of Lens.

The 'Shot at Dawn' campaign to obtain a pardon for those executed for capital crimes in the First World War has given the subject some necessary publicity. The author and lecturer, Julian Putkowski, has been a tenacious and powerful advocate for redress for what appears to be a series of senseless executions. It was Judge Anthony Babington, an unusual and courageous man, who first studied the courts martial and used legal expertise to uncover faults and weaknesses. His book, *For the Sake of Example: Capital Courts-Martial, 1914–1920*, reviews the trials in retrospect on behalf of some of those who were executed.

Field Marshal Lord Carver was of the opinion that the executions were one of the gruesome aspects of the war. I concur with his view, and what I believe to be Judge Babington's, that the trials were generally perfunctory and that the medical evidence, which should have been taken into consideration, was often inadequate and presented *after* the conviction. Lord Carver also points out that the intermediate authorities, that is, the various hierarchies through which the file passed on its route to the commander-in-chief, made recommendation for mercy in a very large number of cases. However, almost invariably, the c-in-c followed the line of one army commander who wrote on a file: 'If toleration is shown to private soldiers who deliberately decline to face danger, all the qualities we desire will be debased and degraded.'

Some stories of boy soldiers are not without controversy. One concerns the young Irishman, Private John Condon. It needs to be examined for what it tells us about the terrible consequences of the brutal business of fighting in the Flanders mud.

The Republic of Ireland is now a confident and prospering country. The darkness of the Troubles is diminishing, though the pain still lingers. One symbol of her national pride and confidence is the view her people are commencing to take of those who volunteered to fight in British uniforms in the First World War. In particular, the city of Waterford's renewed interest in its boy soldier, John Condon, is a heart-warming example. It is through the medium of a play produced by the city's Red Kettle Theatre Company that reconciliation is developing. The company itself describes the play thus:

Red Kettle Theatre Company are proud to present a new play based on the story of John Condon, the youngest allied soldier killed in the First World War and a native of Ballybricken, Waterford. John Condon was just 14 years of age when he was killed during the second battle of Ypres, on the 24th May 1915 – the first time gas was used in warfare. This exciting and theatrical new work tells the story of this ordinary young fella – that walked the same streets as ourselves and found himself, with many more Irishmen, in some of the most horrendous places imaginable – living trench life – facing death on a scale unseen before or since. Men and boys – many of whom believed they were fighting for Home Rule, many no doubt there for the adventure and many there due to their economic situation – but for whatever reasons – they were our neighbours, our cousins, our families and for reasons that had very little to do with them they have been ignored in the telling of our history – even denied their 'Irishness' – forgotten.

At last the Irishness of those who fought in British uniforms can be remembered. John Condon is one symbol of them, wherever the dispute, and there is one, about his age and his grave. To untangle the story we need to look back with care. In 1922 King George V promised 'graves of the [war] dead will be honoured for all time' and for almost ninety years the Commonwealth War Graves Commission has fulfilled his wish. It now cares for 1.7 million graves at 23,000 locations in 150 countries. Each individual British and Commonwealth soldier is remembered without distinction of civil or military rank, race or creed. The name, age and the personal inscription etched on each headstone or panel is the clearest reminder of the human cost of war.[8]

Among the huge number of graves, one visited more often than most is in the Poelcapelle British War Cemetery about 10km north-east of Ypres on the Brugseweg N313. The headstone is marked 6322 Private J. Condon, Royal Irish Regiment, 24th May 1915, Age 14. It is easy to find. Visitors lay tributes around it to commemorate one of the youngest Allied soldiers killed in the war. The collision of myth and history is nowhere more apparent, or more troublesome, than here.

Poelcapelle British War Cemetery was principally set up for the reburial of the remains of British and Commonwealth war dead exhumed from a number of small cemeteries and isolated graves constructed during the course of the Battles of Ypres. There are now 7,478 Commonwealth servicemen of the First World War buried or commemorated there. 6,321 of the burials are unidentified but special memorials commemorate eight casualties known or believed to be buried among them. Other special memorials commemorate twenty-four servicemen buried by the Germans in other locations in the area and whose graves could not be located. The 6,321 unidentified burials need some explanation so that we can illuminate the disputes surrounding John Condon.

The First Battle of Ypres, which commenced on 18 October 1914, was an unsuccessful attempt by the German Army to remove the British from the Ypres Salient in order to break through to the North Sea and the Channel ports. On 23 October, 1,500 German dead were counted on the battlefield around Langemarck. Many were untried troops, including a number of student volunteers. Legend has it that the Germans went into battle singing *Deutschland Uber Alles*. Thereafter, and especially during the Third Reich, the dead of Langemarck came to symbolise the ultimate ideal of self-sacrifice to the German people. Myth was used in the service of militarism.

German hopes of reaching the sea were just as unachievable as the Allied hopes of pushing the enemy out of Belgium. The Battle of Ypres became a conflict for the Salient itself, an area no more than eight miles across at its widest. The Second Battle of Ypres, between 22 April and 25 May 1915, can be subdivided into four conflicts: the Battle of Gravenstafel (22–23 April); the Battle of St Juliaan (24 April–4 May); the Battle of Frezenberg (8–13 May); and the Battle of Bellewaerde (24–25 May). In all, the British suffered 60,000 casualties and the Germans 34,933. The Third Battle of Ypres was fought between 31 July and 10 November 1917 and bears the terrible name of Passchendaele. It finally ended with the Allies gaining four and a half miles of ground for the loss of 66,000 lives – eight killed for every yard gained. The Germans lost about 400,000.[9]

And so it was that thousands of men of the British and Commonwealth armies marched out of the city of Ypres through the Menenpoort onto the Menin Road on their way to the Ypres Salient, never to return. It is fitting, therefore, that the Menin Gate should become a special memorial to the missing. Over the gate to the south stairs are these words:

Here are recorded the names of officers and men who fell in the Ypres salient but to whom the fortunes of war denied the known and honoured burial given to their comrades in death.

The names of 57,896 officers and men are carved in memorial panels.

Father and mother they put aside,
And nearer love also –
An hundred thousand men that died
Whose graves shall no man know.

Thus wrote Rudyard Kipling in his poem 'The King's Pilgrimage'. He knew what he was rhyming about, for his son John, a boy just turned eighteen, had been killed at Chalk Pit Wood on 27 September 1915 during the Battle of Loos. According to the Commonwealth War Graves Commission, John's mortal remains have been found. To others, who dispute that the remains are those of John, he is among 'those who have no grave where any heart can mourn', as his father wrote.

There were many ways of death for a soldier in the Ypres Salient. He might have been shot by a sniper, blown up by a shell explosion, suffocated in a dugout by the fumes of a coal fire, buried in a collapsed trench, gassed, bayoneted, or drowned in glutinous mud. Sometimes bodies were identified and buried by comrades. Sometimes they were left behind during an advance and buried by Allied soldiers, in which case identification was not so easy. Sometimes they were buried by the enemy, having been left in a retreat, in which case identification would have been cursory at least. Those sucked into the mud were left where they were, unmarked and unidentified because it was too dangerous to try to rescue them. Bodies were blown apart by explosions and the bits were collected for burial. Many bodies were simply not found.

When they could, unit chaplains were expected to register the dead and see that their graves were marked. They were responsible for filling in a form with the man's name, number and unit, if the body was identifiable, and had to give a map reference or a good description of the locality. However, burial grounds were often destroyed by shell-fire or otherwise in the ebb and flow of battle, so that large numbers were lost, some for good.

The process of burying the dead in a battlefield was difficult and must have done awful things to the minds of those soldiers who were detailed for the job. The intense nature of the battle meant that the corpses of both sides lay around together until a suitable lull in the fighting allowed burial parties to go to work. James Norman Hall, an American volunteer, wrote of his experience on a burial party. His attempts to capture the accents of his cockney mates are meant for an American readership and appear somewhat exotic. He was in a trench in the rain:

> … I sat on the firing-bench with my head drawn down between my knees watching the water dripping from the edges of my puttees … I had forgotten one important item in the daily routine: supper. And I had

forgotten Private Lemley, our cook ... 'Ere you are, me lads! Bully beef rissoles an' 'ot tea, an' it ain't 'arf bad fer the trenches if I do s'y it.' I can only wonder now at the keenness of our appetites in the midst of the most gruesome surroundings. Dead men were lying about us, both in the trenches and outside of them. And yet our rissoles were not a whit the less enjoyable on that account. It was quite dark when we had finished. The sergeant jumped to his feet. 'Let's get at it, boys,' he said. Half an hour later we erected a wooden cross in Tommy's grave-strewn garden. It bore the following inscription written in pencil: Pte. 4326 MacDonald, Pte 7864 Gardener, Pte 9851 Preston, Pte. 6840 Allen. Royal Fusiliers – They did their bit.[10]

Hostilities ceased, of course, and efforts were intensified to make sense of the huge number of battlefield graves and to locate and identify as many of the monstrous number of dead as possible. Exhumation companies of the Imperial War Graves Commission went to work in the battlefields and a systematic search commenced. The killing fields were divided into manageable units, called grids, which were searched diligently. At least six searches were made on each grid. It was impossible to dig up the whole area, so a number of techniques were developed to find the remains. For example, when bodies decay they release nitrates which turn grass dark green. Shallow burial places are, therefore, identifiable by characteristic dark green patches in grass fields. Sometimes improvised grave markers remained above the ground, with bits of kit such as helmets still attached to them. Soil movements, cultivation or digging animals brought bones and artefacts to the surface. In some cases, locals, who had returned to their homes, were aware of burials and could lead the exhumation companies to the graves.

When graves were found, identification of the remains commenced. It is important to remind ourselves that many of the techniques used today to identify bodies were not then available. Popular television programmes have taught us much about forensic archaeology, which benefits from extensive and growing libraries of digitalised records. In the First World War and immediately afterwads, even dental records were scattered and sketchy, as dental care was less often sought than it is today. DNA was unknown, let alone in use as a forensic tool.

The human remains were placed in creosote-soaked canvass body bags for identification. If any uniform survived, the pockets were searched for personal items such as cigarette cases with inscriptions or identifying marks scratched into them or fragments of letters which may not have decayed. Brass or other metal artefacts, stamped with service numbers, were often found. Boots and leather equipment were more resistant to decay than cloth and often had service and unit numbers marked on them. Where the skull or jawbone remained intact, dental records were made in an effort to match them with any at home.

Once some clues had been identified, they were recorded and the long business of matching the data to a possible name began, while the remains were moved to one of the large central cemeteries for internment. It would have taken a great deal of patience to match the clues from the field to the service records. The first step was to narrow the search by establishing which units had fought in the area of the battlefield grave. The relevant battalion records were searched to match the clues to a likely candidate who had been reported missing, believed dead. Often these efforts were successful, in which case the next of kin would be informed and personal items found on the remains would be forwarded to them. Even then there were complications. Some men had used false names and ages when enlisting. Sometimes it was found that two soldiers had the same service number. It is not surprising that the number of unmarked graves is high.

It appears that some time in the late summer of 1923 an Exhumation Unit of the Imperial War Graves Commission removed the remains from ten unmarked graves at map reference Sheet 28 N.W. square I. 11.b.15.45. This is near what was known on the British maps as 'Railway Wood', which abuts the crossing of a railway line and 'Cambridge Road'. The remains were reburied at Poelcapelle and the grave sites and artefacts found with them were recorded on a Burial Return by the assistant registration officer for No. 1 Area, I.W.G.C. Of those listed, nine of the ten are recorded in the first instance as 'unknown British soldiers'.

In one case, the regimental particulars are shown as '6322 Unknown British Soldier 4/RIR'. In the 'Means of Identification' column are typed the words 'Clothing & Boots stpd. 6322. 4/R.I.R'. In the 'Were any effects forwarded to base?' column are typed the words 'Yes. Piece of Boot'. Later, someone has crossed out the typed words 'Unknown British Solider' and added, in ink, the words 'Pte. J. Condon 2/Roy Irish Rgt. KIA 24/8/15'.[11]

The number 6322 stamped on the clothing and boot was the service number of Private John Condon of the Royal Irish Regiment. It appears that it was on this evidence that the identification was made. According to some sources, his service record shows that he joined the 3rd Battalion, Royal Irish Regiment as a special reservist on 24 October 1913, giving his age as eighteen. Special reservists enlisted for six years and, in the event of a general mobilisation, had to accept the possibility of being called up and undergoing all the same conditions as men of the Army Reserve. This meant that it differed from the Territorial Force in that the men could be sent overseas. Their period as a special reservist started with six months' full-time training, paid the same as a regular, and they had three to four weeks training per year thereafter. When war broke out, John Condon would have been eligible to serve in Belgium.

His record is said to show that he was transferred to 2nd Battalion, Royal Irish Regiment, on 16 December 1914 and that he was killed in action near 'Shell Trap Farm' on 24 May 1915. The regimental war diary of the 2nd Battalion, Royal Irish Regiment, records that at 2.20 a.m. on 24 May 1915 the enemy attacked, preceded by the use of gas which overcame many despite the use of respirators and spray. Shell Trap Farm was captured by the enemy, enabling him to enfilade the Royal Irish position of the line, much of which was taken. The diary records that approximately 17 officers and 378 other ranks from this battalion were reported as casualties. Shell Trap Farm, later referred to as Mouse Trap Farm, is some 3km from 28 N.W.11.b.15.45.[12]

The gas attack on Whit Monday, 24 May 1915, was not the first the Germans had launched. They had used gas ineffectively at Neuve Chapelle at the end of October 1914 and in Poland in January 1915. The Whit Monday attack, however, was fearfully successful for the Germans and at least 3,000 British soldiers were gassed. It is assumed that John Condon was one of them.

As we have seen, the boots and clothing found with the remains at 28 N.W.11.b.15.45 were stamped 6322 4/RIR. John Condon was, it seems, a reservist in the 3rd not the 4th Battalion, Royal Irish Regiment. It must also be noted that 'RIR' could stand for Royal Irish Regiment or Royal Irish Rifles. This weakens the evidence on which the original identification was made. Some investigators are of the view that the kit belonged to 6322 Rifleman Patrick Fitzsimons, 2nd Battalion, Royal Irish

Rifles, who, they argue, was killed on 16 June 1915 and who originally enlisted in the 4th Battalion, Royal Irish Rifles – thus 4/RIR. They marshal considerable evidence to support their argument and go on to suggest that the battlefield cemetery at 28 N.W.11.b.15.45 was very close to the starting position of the 2nd Battalion, Royal Irish Rifles, during the Battle of Bellewaerde on 16 June 1915.[13]

Those who challenge the evidence make one further point. They argue that John Condon did not rush off to join Kitchener's New Army at the outbreak of war. He had, they suggest, already joined the 3rd Battalion, Royal Irish Regiment, as a part-time soldier some nine months before the war. That he lied about his age is not disputed. It has become widely accepted that he was fourteen when he was killed and that is the age which appears on his headstone and on the Commonwealth War Grave Commission website. The evidence presented by those who suggest that he was, in fact, nineteen, has not yet convinced the CWGC or the British Ministry of Defence.

Despite this sad and sometimes acrimonious controversy, many of the folk of Waterford have remained constant, as we are also bound to do, with the authorised view of the CWGC. It would, thus, be encouraging to find more evidence to support the claim that John Condon was fourteen when he was killed.

On Monday 10 November 2003, the Irish TV station, RTE 1, screened a programme which told the story of how this young Waterford lad trained for military service in the army barracks in Clonmel, after he fooled a British Army recruiting officer into believing he was eighteen years of age. It appears that John Condon's family only discovered he was in Belgium when they were contacted by the British Army after he went missing in action on 24 May 1915.[14]

Meanwhile, the John Condon story goes on. For many he represents the thousands of Irish boys in the British Army who were killed in the First World War. They deserve recognition on both sides of the Irish Sea.

8

A LAND UNFIT FOR HEROES

You are asked to be silent for two minutes today, to be silent and pause in your labours, to remember this day and this hour and this year ... What will you remember and what will you forget? You will remember, mothers, the sons you have lost; wives, you will think of husbands who went out in the mist of the winter morning – the mist that sent cold chills round the heart – never to come back again. And brothers will think of brothers and friends of friends, all lying dead today under an alien soil.

But what will you forget? The crime that called these men to battle? The war that was to end war and in reality did not?

Make the most of this day of official remembrance. By the sacred memory of those lost to you, swear to yourselves this day at 11 o'clock, that never again, God helping you, shall the peace and happiness of the world fall into the murderous hands of cynical old men.

Front page of the *Daily Herald*, 11 November 1919.

On 8 August 1918 the British, Australian and Canadian forces launched what became known as the Amiens Offensive. By this time, a series of German offensives had petered out nine miles short of the town.

The German Army was shattered in morale, short of men and especially short of trained and experienced leaders. On the other hand, the British had learnt the hard lessons of trench warfare at last. The Amiens Offensive was a carefully planned and very successful combined arms assault. Modern warfare had emerged.

Deception and strict secrecy yielded surprise. Wireless communication, although still in its infancy, was in use and the Allies achieved the great intelligence coup of being able to read the German signals – a small but significant precursor of the Enigma story of the next war. The infantry was supported by considerable firepower in the form of Lewis guns, mortars, machine guns and smoke grenades. Ninety-five per cent of the German guns had been identified by new techniques invented in 1917 and were quickly put out of action by British artillery. This meant that the German counter-preparations were nullified. Around 1,900 aircraft quickly gained air supremacy and disguised the arrival of 534 tanks at the start line. The British attack was assisted by mist and smoke, which covered the 4.20 a.m. start, and the German relief rotation which had started during the night was incomplete, leaving their defences undermanned.

The attack was successful, advancing up to eight miles on the first day. The next day further advances were made but the cost was high. Tanks and aircraft were destroyed in large numbers. The attack ended on 11 August but it had made a disproportionate impression on the Germans and they acknowledged it as the greatest defeat their army had suffered since the beginning of the war.[1]

The Amiens Offensive was the beginning of the end and the German front began to disintegrate. Further British and Allied offensives, using similar battlefield management techniques, led to the smashing of the Hindenburg Line. With her army falling back, Germany signed an armistice on 11 November 1918. Characteristically, the British prefer to forget the great victories of 1918 but treasure the memories of the Somme and Passchendaele.

Then there were the ex-prisoners of war, so often forgotten now. In the *Reading School Magazine* dated April 1918 this notice appeared:

On Wednesday in last week Captain Fielding Clarke of Amphill, Craven Rd, Reading, received a telegram intimating that his second son, Second Lieutenant A. Fielding Clarke, RFC, was missing. The previous Saturday he had been with his squadron carrying out a bombing raid on and around Metz and his machine was the only one which did not return. Lieut. Clarke, whose age is 18 years and 6 months, was educated at Reading School and Bradfield College, and joined the RFC at the age of 17 years and four months. He had been in France about three months and had just returned from his first furlough. It is supposed that the cause of his failing to return must have been engine trouble, for on the occasion of the raid there was particularly little German anti-aircraft fire. Lieut. A. Fielding Clarke is known to be a prisoner of war interned at Karlsruhe.

Fielding Clarke survived the war and we later hear that he became an interesting figure at St John's College, Oxford, from whence someone mentioned him very briefly in a letter to one of his old schoolmasters. It is a telling little sentence, redolent of eccentricity and humour, and as unlike as it might be from the anguished lines of the war poets. It reads:

A.F. Clarke ... still carries his pocket violin (as at school) and proves that music hath charms to soothe the savage breast.

Perhaps Fielding Clarke was able to look upon his brief experience as a prisoner of war as part of the adventure of war.

Aviation played an important part in the outcome of the war, though how significant it was is even now a matter of debate. By 1918 there were more than 8,000 aircraft on all sides at the Western Front and, as we have seen, the side with air supremacy was able to exercise control over the battle as never before. Fielding Clarke was a bomber pilot. When he was shot down, he was attempting to attack the strategic railway infrastructure around Metz.

In April 1918 the first autonomous air arm, the Royal Air Force, was formed by Lloyd George's government. Some say he encouraged its formation so that he might exercise some strategic control over at least one arm of the forces, since he had been notably unsuccessful in his intrigues against Haig. By the end of the war, the British were poised to bomb Berlin with the giant Handley-Page V-500. Here we see the commencement of modern strategic bombing, which ended in the much-debated devastation of Dresden, the equally lethal fire-storm of Tokyo and the eventual release of atomic weapons over Hiroshima and Nagasaki in the Second World War.

It is pertinent to ask if the terror bombing campaign launched by the RFC, and its successor, the RAF, made an impact in 1918. By a strange coincidence, there appeared in the *Reading School Magazine* of July 1919 the report of a talk about his experiences by Captain Revd A.G. Wilkinson, brigade chaplain, Canadian Force. He had returned to Britain after a year and eighteen months as a prisoner of war in Gutersloh, Minden, Crefeld, Schwarmstedt, Holminden and Freiburg camps. He was an angry man who used emotive language to convey his distress but there is no reason to question his veracity. The report reads in part:

> It was satisfactory to hear of the abject terror inspired in the frontier towns by our air raids, though sad to think that our own poor fellows were too often deliberately exposed, in reprisal camps such as Freiburg, to the awful destruction. These deadly air raids of ours, ever drawing nearer and nearer, were a great factor in bringing the war to a speedy conclusion.

A further investigation showed that the Reverend Wilkinson was trying to draw attention to an apparent war crime which, he may have felt, justified the British terror bombing. In this he foreshadows L. Van Der Post and others who argued that the destruction of Hiroshima and Nagasaki was defensible because it ensured that thousands of Allied POWs in Japanese hands were not executed by their captors as the Second World War drew to a conclusion. Here is Wilkinson writing in December 1918 for the *Chevrons and Stars*, the magazine of the Canadian training base at Bexhill-on-Sea:

> It was Thursday morning, February 16th last year, and intensely cold, the thermometer registered 10 degrees below zero. At 9 a German soldier came to tell me that I was wanted at the camp hospital. I was there met by the British doctor, Capitan Frank Park, C.A.M.C., who told me that sixteen British prisoners had just arrived from the station seven kilometres away. With him I went to Ward 2, and there saw 16 specimens of humanity. That is all I could call them, 16 frozen hollow cheeked wrecks, the remnants of hundreds and hundreds of once strong healthy men, who had been taken prisoner and had been kept to work behind the lines. Their comrades were dead.
>
> Now these men were captured in September, October and November, 1916, and kept to work close up to the front working in preparation for

the big German retreat planned to take place in February and March, 1917. Their work was demolishing houses, bridges, felling trees, making roads and digging trenches, those called the Hindenburg line. This line and others were built by prisoners of war. We praised German engineering skill and paid silent tribute to the endurance of the German working parties, but it was not the work of the German parties but the work of prisoners, Russians, Rumanians in thousands, tens of thousands, and of British. They worked under appalling conditions, brutal treatment, blows, kicks, death if they refused, with housing and quarters not fit for pigs and food not enough to keep body and soul together. What did it matter if they died, there were plenty more where they came from? Germany numbered her prisoners by millions. Prisoners they were, not prisoners-of-war; slaves, yea worse than slaves.

These details these poor wretches told us with tears in their eyes when they spoke of some poor dear friend and pal who died beside them at work, died of exposure, starvation or our own shell fire. They told us of the clothes they had to wear. There was no need to tell, we saw for ourselves when we undressed them. Here is the list, and think of the temperature and cold as you read it: thin service tunic and trousers, old cotton shirt, socks and boots, and an old cap. That was all, no warm underclothing, no great coat. All these the Boche had stolen under the plea that they had to be fumigated.

And what did the outside world know or care? It may have cared, it must have cared, but it knew nothing. Germany took good care of that. These men were reported in the British Casualty Lists as missing and missing they will remain till the end of time. I reported them to the Record Offices of their Regiments and my letters never got home. This was just one isolated instance of many that might be quoted.

The prisoners of war were eventually repatriated. However, the process of demobilising the new armies was beset by serous difficulties. It had been taken over by a committee of the Ministry of Reconstruction and was mired in the awful tangle common to insensitive bureaucracies. Demobilisation did not commence until 9 December 1918. The majority of soldiers found this very hard to stomach, since the war effectively ended when the Armistice was signed on 11 November 1918.

Those of us familiar with the distortions and frustrations caused by over-centralised government will understand immediately when we hear that the plan was devised by a civilian committee and military advice was largely ignored. It was predicated on the contribution individuals were thought to be capable of making to the needs of industry and the economy. A laudable effort to release married men with long service records and those who had been in battle for long periods was built into the plan but it had the effect of complicating things.

The first men to be released were those who were to be involved in the demobilisation process itself. Next were to be the pivotal men, who were selected because they were thought to be capable of creating employment for others. These were to be followed into civilian life by soldiers who could produce a slip from an employer stating that there was a job awaiting them. There was a fourth category of those whose pre-war employment had been of national importance. The fifth group, in which men were to be released according to the importance of their profession or trade, came last. It hardly needs saying but those who had joined the army straight from school stood little chance of getting home until very late in the process. The scheme was inequitable and corruptible. It was further complicated because it was administered by fourteen government departments and thus open to administrative delay and error.[2]

Lloyd George had taken his eye off the ball. He was concentrating on the election, which he had called to capitalise on the military victory. Trouble arose quickly and recriminations began to appear in the press. Hindsight shows us that the real cause of the chaos was the naivety of a group of the bureaucrats who were unable to understand that, once the war was over, the army would lose its raison d'etre and thus discipline would deteriorate rapidly.

There was, for some time, real work for almost a million troops to dismantle the trappings of war in France and Belgium. There was also the matter of finding troops for the British Army of the Rhine, which was to occupy Germany for a while. However, there was not enough for everyone to do and there was no point in continuing to train for war. The well-known military tendency to find tedious work for idle soldiers and the diminishing respect for the eccentricities of military discipline led to discontent.

On 3 and 4 January 1919, around 10,000 soldiers at Folkestone and 2,000 at Dover refused to board ships which were to return them to France. There were sympathetic demonstrations in the streets of many large cities in Britain and, in an unprecedented show of discontent, soldiers in uniform drove up and down outside Whitehall waving banners. It all became ugly and caused much unrest. It was also an outrider for the army of bureaucrats, which came to prominence as central government began to wield more power.[3]

Ernest Glaeser argues that there were four generations, of which the first was made up of the conservative ideologists who stoked the war fever. The second consisted of men born around 1890 who had entered the war in adult life. The third group, to which Kitchener's Lost Boys belonged, was the generation that had gone to war straight from school. The last generation was made up of those who were too young to fight in the First World War but were old enough to compete with the Lost Boys for their place in society.[4]

The Lost Boys had survived appalling experiences and many found that their dreams of a heroic reception, when they eventually got home, were dashed. The French author Drieu de la Rochelle, who later became notorious during the Second World War for his unfortunate collaboration with the occupying Germans, called them 'poor children, fascinating but lost.' Some expatriates living in postwar France attached the famous tag 'The Lost Generation' to this notably hedonistic group. Ernest Hemingway, who was prominent among them, having gone early to the war as a volunteer ambulance driver with the Italians, wrote about the growing disenchantment with war and the frenetic effort to suppress bad memories.

They had known no adult life before the war and were, as Vera Brittain wrote, 'the lost youth the war had stolen.' Their plight was summed up by the war poet Robert Graves:

> Not only did I have no experience of independent civilian life, having gone straight from school into the army: I was still mentally and nervously organised for war. Shells used to come bursting on my bed at midnight … Strangers in daytime would assume the faces of friends who had been killed.[5]

Robert von Ranke Graves was the very model of the Lost Boys. His life story is well enough known but is worth recapitulating. He was born on 14 July 1895 and was educated at a dame-school and a number of preparatory schools. In 1909 he entered Charterhouse, where he was bullied. He found solace in writing poetry and his early work appears in the Charterhouse school magazine. There he formed a friendship with a younger boy, G.H. Johnstone. He was later to describe this relationship as pseudo-homosexual and celebrated it in some of his earlier poems. He left Charterhouse in the summer of 1914, intending to take up a classical exhibition at St John's College, Oxford. While he was on holiday in Wales, the German invasion of Belgium affronted him so much that he volunteered for service immediately, despite his pacifist leanings, and was commissioned into the Royal Welsh Fusiliers.

In 1916 he was so badly wounded in the lung that he was left for dead and had the strange experience of reading his own obituary in *The Times*. He was sent to Craiglockhart hospital suffering from shell-shock in 1917. His attraction to a pretty nurse during his recovery was followed by a revulsion for his old school friend Johnstone, who had been convicted of making homosexual advances. These experiences appear to have focused his sexual orientation and in 1918 he married Annie Mary Pryde, the sister of artist Ben Nicholson. They moved to Oxford, where he took up his exhibition at St John's. However, Graves was still affected by shell-shock and was forced to give up his undergraduate studies; for a while, he lived on handouts from friends. One was the enigmatic hero T.E. Lawrence. His condition affected his wife's health and they left Oxford so he could take up the post of professor of English Literature at Cairo University. His marriage was saved by a relationship with the young American poet Laura Riding, with whom he lived in a *ménage à trois* with his wife. Later, the Irish poet Geoffrey Phibbs joined them in a strange *ménage à quatre* for a while.

After that, with Laura in tow but without Annie, Graves moved to Majorca where he had a productive period of writing. Laura left him and Graves returned to England, again being saved from a breakdown by meeting Beryl Hodge, with whom he moved to Devon for the duration of the Second World War.

In 1945 Graves returned to Majorca, this time with Hodge. His reputation grew apace and in 1971 he was made an honorary fellow of St John's College. He continued to find the company of beautiful women necessary for his artistic life and his muses included the artist Judith Bledsoe and the ballet dancer Julia Simon. He died in Majorca in 1985. Apart from his war poetry, his literary output was prolific. He is probably best known to the general public for his novels *I, Claudius* and *Claudius the God*.[6]

Graves was one of many. Over 80,000 cases of shell-shock were treated during the First World War. Despite the advances in treating the condition, it was not always sympathetically perceived among those with little or no operational experience. The strange stigma died hard and still survived in the latter part of the twentieth century. Chronic symptoms were sometimes attributed by laymen to the effects of syphilis or alcoholism. Common names for it, such as 'funk', sum up the scorn with which it was viewed in the services. The proper term for the condition was 'War Strain' and thus it was better understood or defined as the mental effects of war experiences which were sufficient to incapacitate a man from the performance of his military duties. When officers started to succumb to War Strain, it began to be recognised as a legitimate medical disorder. The ratio of shell-shocked officers to other ranks was a staggering one to six.[7]

The state of mind of a young soldier after a mine explosion, being buried in a dugout or seeing and hearing his wounded and mangled comrades was generally ameliorated by military discipline and the presence of familiar comrades-in-arms. It is common for men in combat to control the outward signs of fear, such as tremors, twitching, and loss of control of the facial and vocal muscles, so as to give the appearance of calm. With practice and by 'consuming his own smoke', he may be able to appear even calmer, more in control, more contemptuous of danger than before.

Suppressing the external signs of fear is achieved by controlling the skeletal muscles via the voluntary nervous system. What very few ordinary people are able to do is suppress the autonomic nervous system, which regulates the respiratory, circulatory, digestive and excretory systems. Thus extreme cases are unable to control their bladder or anal sphincter.

Training would have done much to prepare a soldier mentally and physically to face the military causes of fear and anxiety. That is one of its major functions today and the reason it appears harsh to civilians at times. The military understand that this means suppressing anger and frustration, which need an outlet if good mental health is to be maintained. They deal with the problem by encouraging soldiers to play hard during spare time. Rugby, football and boxing help to release suppressed tension, as do wild mess games which do much to relieve the tension of command among young officers.

How a soldier survived in the trenches will have depended on the nature, duration, intensity and frequency of frightening events, and on factors such as remorse for major or minor errors, anger, elation and the fear of being afraid. Few people have been called upon to suppress fear for so long and in such unique circumstances as the combat soldiers of the Great War.

In natural fighting the enemy is visible. The intense excitement of the fight is for a short duration and the emotion of fear is soon suppressed. In trench warfare the conditions were different. The enemy was largely unseen and the frequent artillery assaults he made were impersonal, indiscriminate and unpredictable. The noise of approaching missiles, the bursting shells, the screams of the injured assailed the man in the trench while he was fighting for self-control. The release of pent-up emotion was not possible. Sleep deprivation for long periods was a debilitating factor, as was the tendency to feel sympathetic pain, distress, disgust or nausea at the happenings in the trenches. Under normal conditions, fear is a useful emotion. In the unnatural conditions of trench warfare, fear was held in check for far too long.

So it was that many soldiers collapsed when a shell burst near them and, though they may not have been physically injured or unconscious, they were removed from the trenches dazed or delirious, with twitching, trembling and loss of muscular power. Some soldiers were struck blind, deaf or mute and, in rare cases, all three at once or successively. These symptoms often vanished as quickly and as dramatically as they had appeared. Sometimes men found that they were unable to unclench a fist or that their backs were bent at right angles to their limbs. These strange contractions took much longer to disappear.

There were, however, invisible manifestations of war strain. They were common to thousands of patients who found their way to hospitals, and probably to many thousands more who were not diagnosed and treated. The symptoms were loss of memory, terrifying dreams, insomnia, low self-esteem, obsessive thoughts, pains and sometimes hallucinations. All of these, of course, are now known to be those of post-traumatic shock syndrome and often occurred some time after the soldier had left the scene of combat. Therefore, many sufferers may never have sought treatment.

Repression plays an important part in training for combat. Soldiers are required to act calmly and methodically in the presence of grave danger.

Their training normally takes years. The soldiers of Kitchener's new armies were trained for six months at the most. To add to the severity of the problem, the British service tradition was to banish terrible memories, make light of death and destruction and thrust bad thoughts aside. This form of repression was dubbed the 'stiff upper lip' and it was, and still is, doubly dangerous for long-term mental health.

There is no way of telling how many soldiers suffered from delayed symptoms. The most recognisable low-level symptom of the problem was morbid irritability. Sufferers became upset, took offence rapidly and became very difficult to live with. They were unable to talk about their wartime experiences with their families and became irritated if pressed to do so. Years after the war many veterans complained of frequent nightmares and hallucinations. No doubt many turned to drink and not a few became violent when in their cups. An unknown number of families became battle grounds and the effect on children and grandchildren is incalculable. Anyone who has experience of mental illness in a family will know that the collateral damage is enormous and sustained from generation to generation.

The neurophysiological changes which take place in the brain during adolescence have been discussed briefly in an earlier chapter. It would be interesting – and relevant today – to determine if the long-term effects of War Strain were different in victims whose brain development was still incomplete. As Peter Simkins pointed out in his book *Kitchener's Army*, some soldiers were very young indeed. He quotes Randal Sidebotham writing in the *North Cheshire Herald* in 1916, who states that Harry Whittaker of Hyde in Cheshire was only thirteen years and eight months old when he volunteered for service in the 2/6th Cheshire Regiment in November 1914. As we have seen, the brain does not complete its developmental processes until the age of nineteen and, thus, the conscript armies of 1916, with their predominance of eighteen-year-old boys, will have been interesting in this context.

As an illustration of the long-term effect of this debilitating problem, it is worth remembering that over 65,000 men still remained in hospital suffering from shell-shock in 1927. The author's father-in-law administered the Royal Naval Hospital, Great Yarmouth, in which a good number of First World War shell-shock victims were still being treated in the sixties and later. The quality of nursing was not up to modern standards and patients were often the victims of callous ridicule.

Many were there until they died, some never having a visit from a relative, possibly because their families were unable to face mental illness which was often feared and looked down upon.

Demobilised soldiers who had reached the higher levels of public school education were able to resume their academic careers. They lived in a sympathetic society which was able to understand their mental health problems. Those boys without university places to go to or family businesses to join were forced to seek work.

For ex-servicemen, returning to civilian life is a difficult experience at any time. In the case of those with recent experience of combat, there was a strange inability to adapt to the petty concerns of ordinary domestic and workplace life, where established hierarchies and relationships were strong. Men with experience of making life or death decisions found it hard to adapt to the orders of their civilian supervisors. The peer group bonds formed in the trenches were very strong indeed and were probably best replicated in civilian life by the male, boozy, classless camaraderie of the pub. The sense of constant danger suddenly stopped and the urge to recreate it was paradoxically powerful. This led to reckless behaviour which tested the law.

The boy soldier who ate his first civilian breakfast in his family home may have appeared to his mother as the same lad who went blithely to war in 1914 – but he was really someone else. He had missed four years of those small but crucial events in the narrow world of his village or street. Young men near his own age would have usurped his expected position and would be unwilling to relinquish their place in the social hierarchy. If he had joined the army straight from school, he would have had no previous work experience to offer and would have had to start work alongside recent school leavers – if he could find a job. What were his prospects?

A story told to the author by an anonymous old friend will help to make things clear. His father volunteered for service at the age of seventeen in an Irish regiment early in the war. He went to the front as a private soldier and was severely wounded in the chest. He recalled that the stretcher bearers carrying him to the dressing station were discussing his case and deciding that he was too badly injured to worry about. They were about to jettison him from the stretcher when his young subaltern, who had been following the stretcher, threatened them with his pistol if they did not continue. They did so. He survived but was unfit for front-line service.

He joined the Army Service Corps as a driver and served out the war. When he was discharged he returned to his family, by now in London, and tried to find work. He found nothing.

He took to cycling around the neighbourhood factories, offering himself for casual labour. One day he entered a small factory and asked for work. The manager let him clean the windows, which had long since needed attention. There were so many windows that he was asked to continue until the job was done. More casual work was found for him and he was eventually taken on as permanent. He stayed with the factory and slowly built up a reputation and finally, after many years, became its manager. Similar stories are easy to find but it should be noted that the old soldier in question had received a gallantry award for the action which led to his wounding. His postwar employment depended on his own dogged persistence, not upon the efforts of a government bureaucrat who had sat behind a desk for forty years and had hung his hat on a pension.

For many returning soldiers it was not to be the land fit for heroes that Lloyd George had so eloquently proposed. By the end of 1920 it was estimated that 20,000 ex-officers were out of work. Earl Haig asserted that about 3,000 of them were disabled and trying to live on a pension of a mere £70 per year. He pointed out that this was half of an agricultural labourer's wage and did not compare favourably with the £2 per week paid first to other ranks, especially since such a large number of officers had been commissioned from the ranks. By the summer of 1921 the postwar slump reached its peak, with 2.5 million unemployed. The veteran soldier's position is summarised in this quotation from Phillip Gill's novel, *Young Anarchy*. The character Frank Hardy, the unemployed veteran of the novel, states:

> You see, we fellows who went through it all had grown four years older without learning anything about peace-time jobs. We missed the boat, so to speak. The younger crowd had filled up the places, and left us stranded.

It is likely that much of the burden of helping unemployed ex-servicemen fell on the voluntary organisations. They were, at first, heavily politicised. The first off the mark was the National Association of Discharged Sailors and Soldiers. This was formed in September

1916 and was widely known as the Association. Its formation had been encouraged and assisted by the trade unions and the Labour Party. It was very much against allowing ex-officers to join. Next came the National Federation of Discharged and Demobilised Sailors and Soldiers. It was formed in April 1917 and was associated with the Liberal Party. This was known as the Federation and it barred officers who had not been commissioned from the ranks from joining.

A third organisation called Comrades of the Great War was formed as a counterweight to the Association and the Federation by some Conservative MPs and others in August 1917. Membership of the Comrades was open to all ranks. The National Union of Ex-Service Men was formed in 1919 but its radical leanings were alarming and it was blighted by its later association with the British Union of Fascists. The Officers' Association was not formed until January 1920.

The political nature of most of these organisations was not helpful and it became clear that a unified approach would serve the needs of ex-servicemen better. In June 1919 the British Legion was formed and, despite the many machinations of the politically minded, it became the major ex-servicemen's organisation and remains strong today. It has been closely associated with Earl Haig, who was its first president, and it has been subject to some criticism as a result.[8]

The New Army training emphasised peer bonding rather than class bonding. Many observers argue that this was a major factor holding the army together in 1917 and 1918, when the pre-war ideology failed. This meant that public schoolboys bonded with men they would never have met on the same scale before the war. As more and more officers were commissioned from the ranks, some of the rigid class barriers began to break down. But the class structure was particularly resilient in Britain and the claims that it was shattered by the war were, I suspect, premature. It had, however, been challenged by a middle class growing in confidence, and the unthinking deference which paralysed social mobility before the war was undermined. Many thousands of adolescents had been given positions of authority and had lived through experiences which made them determined not to revert to their pre-war state of near invisibility. The age of adolescence can, with some certainty, be said to have its origin in the First World War.

Politics certainly changed after the war, though it may be said fairly that they had been on hold for much of it. The rise in trade union power was noticeable immediately. The unions had been involved in the huge industrial changes needed to manufacture armaments. They had been included in local committees which tried to set wages and distribute labour, in return for agreeing to conscription, wage control and the employment of women. The issue of conscription had been particularly contentious, as we have seen, and major strikes were threatened as a protest against it in the late summer of 1915. Further shop-floor trade union action resulted in strikes in the engineering industry in 1916 and 1917.

The unions had achieved considerable power as a result of all this and it was said that some of them refused to assist in the retraining of ex-soldiers because they feared job losses for their members would result. In January 1919 the government apparently perceived that a triple alliance of railway, coal-mining and transport unions would strike in order to establish a socialist state. A general strike which broke out in September 1919 was troublesome, since the police force was undermanned and demoralised. Fortunately, it ended in November 1920 but it left deep social rifts unhealed. The army had been on standby to come to the aid of the civil power. This was never a good thing in Britain.

The absence of fathers and big brothers had stripped many urban areas of traditional authority figures and the increase in work for women had further deprived children of regular home routine. In addition, the school-leaving age was relaxed in many cases to allow children from the age of thirteen to work where the need arose. Thus the normal social structure which held families in shape was undermined. This led to the development of gangs, in which the adolescent need for peer bonding was exploited. Youth crime increased, as did the interest of the press in the more lurid events. It is doubtful if the traditional male authority figures were able to re-establish themselves in households, especially where men returned suffering from debilitating wounds, mental or physical. It was, therefore, an uneasy street to which many young soldiers returned on demobilisation.

It has been estimated that 3 million people, out of a total population of 42 million, lost close relatives during the war. This figure only includes what are called 'primary bereaved', that is immediate family.[9] If one includes 'secondary bereaved', that is cousins, uncles, friends and so on, the figure becomes enormous. Jane Shilling, in *The Times* of 6 June 2008, wrote of a subject which filled the post-First World War establishment with foreboding. According to the 1921 census, there were 1.75 million spinsters in Britain. They were known with some objectivity but little humanity as 'The Surplus Women'. Shilling tells us that they were depicted in *Punch* cartoons as 'pathetic gooseberries, awkwardly perched in their droopy knitwear between their luckier sisters who had contrived to snag a man.' Virginia Nicholson's study of the post-First World War spinsters in her book *Singled Out* discusses this issue which has, so far, received less than its rightful attention. The following quote drives the point home with force and clarity:

> 'Girls,' said the senior mistress of Bournemouth High School for Girls to her sixth form in 1917, 'I have come to tell you a terrible fact. Only one in ten of you can ever hope to marry. This is not a guess ... It is a statistical fact. Nearly all the men who might have married you have been killed. You will have to make your way in the world as best you can.'[10]

Illustrative is the case of Vera Brittain, who wrote *Testament of Youth* in 1933, and had lost her fiancé, her brother and two of her closest male friends during the war.

The disproportionate number of officers killed in the war had long-term effects. Firstly, those who were commissioned came largely from literate classes which, by 1914, had become the literate masses. Teachers, artists, lawyers, writers, poets and historians had volunteered in droves and were mown down likewise. Their loss to the communities as a whole is incalculable. This was different to other wars in which Britain had engaged. The pre-war army had been officered by the aristocracy and soldiered by the very poor. Indeed, the old army was just about the only welfare organisation available in peacetime for the out of work and the unemployable. Since the middle classes were not involved, the British colonial wars tended to be fought at one remove from most people. The nasty deaths and appalling injuries were confined to those who were too rich or too poor to matter a lot. Kipling's poem about Tommy Atkins says it all:

> Then it's Tommy this, an' Tommy that, an' 'Tommy 'ow's yer soul?'
> But it's 'Thin red line of 'eroes' when the drums begin to roll –

> For it's Tommy this, an' Tommy that, an' 'Chuck him out, the brute!'
> But it's 'Saviour of 'is country' when the guns begin to shoot.

The new armies brought the war home to the middle classes. The need to understand it and to find someone to blame was thus more insistent and acute. The war poets gained in popularity and their interpretation of the war became proportionally more important and tended to distract from a proper analysis of events. Even now, despite our great advances in gathering real-time intelligence, the fog of war quickly descends on a battlefield and each survivor tells a different story to the confusion of historians and the glee of politicians. Haste, fatigue and lost documents cloud the judgement of those charged with writing official reports and finding and naming the dead. Dramatists, novelists, film makers and journalists shape and spin the evidence and add a pinch of fiction to leaven their stories. Each medium limits the writer and, therefore, acts as a distorting mirror for the truth. Fame attracts jealousy, bad journalism and careless biographers. The habit of reading history backwards helps no one.

There is a good case for writing about the historiography of the First World War. Indeed, the temptation has been strong during the work on this book. The Second World War took the First off the agenda for a while and the Cold War, and the possibility it engendered of Armageddon, focused the minds of historians for a long time. The First World War politicians, starting with Lloyd George, had been quick to make their case against the generals, and Sir William Robertson, the CIGS, and Haig, the commander in the field, both had their reputations damaged. The pacifist movement surrounding the Vietnam disaster became very powerful and influenced critical appraisal of the 1914–18 war. The emergence of satirical comedy in the sixties found easy targets in generals and staff officers, and the phrases 'Oh What a Lovely War' and 'Lions led by Donkeys' became irresistible tools in the hands of the press. Recent docu-fiction has taken its turn in promoting myth. It becomes harder for historians and laymen alike to be objective.

What then of the Empire and the boy heroes of old? Were they forever outlawed? Not so. The case of Biggles, the fictional aviator, will serve to make the point. The nature of the war in the air threw up new heroes. Mass slaughter on a grand scale had made the individual solider into a statistic. The heroes of the Royal Flying Corps, who pitted themselves in single combat against the Red Baron and his deadly aces, gave the public a much-needed affirmation of the value of the individual. Fighter pilots became the heroes of the First World War; the new military elite drawn from the middle classes – the dashing, the brave and the audacious Lieutenant Daedalus Icarus Brown, pilot of fame and renown.

The ace writer of flying fiction was W.E. Johns. He had seen active service in the trenches at Gallipoli and transferred to the Royal Flying Corps in 1917. He was a member of 55 Squadron and was involved in bombing raids on Germany. He was shot down in 1918 and became a prisoner of war, a not unfamiliar story. The hero of his fiction was Biggles, the nickname of James Bigglesworth. When he was first introduced to the readers by Johns, Bigglesworth was in the Royal Flying Corps. Johns wrote an economical but realistic pen portrait of his hero at that time:

> Bigglesworth, commonly called Biggles, a fair-haired, good looking lad still in his teens, but an active Flight Commander, is talking; not of wine or women as novelists would have us believe, but of a new fusee spring for a Vickers gun which would speed it up another hundred rounds a minute. He had killed a man not six hours before. He had killed six men during the past month – or was it a year, he had forgotten. Time had become curiously telescoped lately. What did it matter anyway? His careless attitude told one story, but the irritating little falsetto laugh which continually punctuated his tale told another.

The early novels of the daring adventures of Biggles were war stories. *The Camels are Coming* appeared in 1932, *Biggles of the Camel Squadron* in 1933 and *Biggles Learns to Fly* in 1935. He was a good hero and his skill and his aircraft set him free to appear in romantic venues all over the world. These included Brazil, for example, in *The Cruise of the Condor* and the South Pacific in *Biggles in the South Seas*. In his adventures he was usually accompanied by his old service mates, the Honourable Algernon Lacey and Flight Sergeant Smyth. Smyth could not shake off his non-commissioned status, it seems. Later, Biggles was accompanied by the fifteen-year-old Ginger Hebblethwaite and the female interest in the person of Flight Officer Joan Worralson of the Women's Auxiliary Air Force. All these characters were projected on the now wider British Empire to outwit dastardly Germans, oily Greeks and wild Pacific islanders. Then, they appeared in Britain, fighting crime with the flying detective, Sergeant Bigglesworth of the CID. By the time Johns died in 1968 he had published 102 books about Biggles. The Suez crisis came and went and, with it, the old Empire, but the adventure still lingered on in juvenile fiction.

After the war, the question of who was responsible for the carnage became insistent. It is worth reiterating the following points: The peacetime British Army had drawn its officers from the upper reaches of the upper classes and its soldiers from the dregs of society. If they were killed, it did not seem to matter much. The First World War was the first in which middle-class Britain experienced heavy casualties and this meant that ordinary people demanded answers.

The politicians wriggled and spun their way out of the firing line and so much of the blame was attributed to the generals and their staff officers. Great military reputations were destroyed. The debate about Haig's performance is still alive. One question which exercises our minds is how he was able to send so many young men to certain death. Lloyd George was concerned about the heavy losses but seems to have been powerless to control Haig. The blame game continues and the media is gleefully but sometimes inaccurately involved. Myths have grown up, so that it is now difficult to root out the truth.

Modern military commanders are influenced by a combination of their own moral values, political oversight and a powerful news media. The First World War occurred at a time of slower communications and a changing attitude to battlefield losses. The Victorian acceptance of death was giving way to the modern denial of death. Haig and his fellow commanders were of the earlier cast. We are firmly of the latter.

As we have seen, many factors were involved but who was to blame in Britain? The answer would appear to be the British people themselves, in the shape of their politicians. For political and financial reasons, they consistently refused to maintain a standing army of conscripts. They also failed to make arrangements to raise and train an army, should the need arise. They even neglected to keep a register of men of military age or account for the manpower requirements of armament factories. Despite this, they blithely went to war against the most efficient and well-trained mass army in the world.

A TIME LINE OF THE MAIN BRITISH ENGAGEMENTS ON THE WESTERN FRONT (1914–1918)

1914

23–24 August	Mons
24 August	Audregnies
26 August	Le Cateau
24 August – 5 September	Retreat from Mons
1 September	Nery
5–10 September	Marne
14–15 September	Aisne
10 October – 2 November	La Bassée
12 October – 2 November	Messines
13 October – 2 November	Armentières
18 October – 12 November	Ypres
21–24 October	Langemarck
25–30 October	Hollebeke Chateau
29–31 October	Gheluvelt
11 November	Nonne Bosschen
23–24 November	Festubert
14 December	Wytschaete
20–21 December	Givenchy

1915

15 January	Givenchy
10–12 March	Neuve Chapelle
17–22 April	Hill 60
22–23 April	Gravenstafel
24 April – 4 May	St Juliaan
8–13 May	Frezenberg
9–17 May	Aubers Ridge
15–25 May	Festubert
24–25 May	Bellewaerde
19, 30 July – 30 Aug	Hooge
25 September – 8 October	Loos
25 September	Bois Grenier
25 September	Pietre

1916

27 March – 16 April	St Eloi Craters
2–13 June	Mount Sorrel
1 July – 18 November	Somme
1–13 July	Albert
1 July	Beaumont Hammel
1 July	Schwaben Redout
14–17 July	Bazentin
15 July – 3 September	Delville Wood
19 July	Fromelles
23 July – 3 September	Pozières
2–28 September	Thiepval
3–6 September	Guillemont
9 September	Ginchy
15–22 September	Flers Courcelette
25–28 September	Morval
1 October – 11 November	Ancre Heights
13–18 November	Ancre

1917

9–14 April	Arras
9–14 April	Vimy Ridge
9–14 April	Scarpe

23–24 April	Scarpe
28–29 April	Arlux
3–4 May	Scarpe
3–17 May	Bullecourt
28 June	Oppy Wood
31 July – 10 November	Ypres
31 July – 2 August	Pilckem
10 August	Westhoek
15–25 August	Hill 70
16–18 August	Langemarck
22–27 August	St Juliaan
20–25 September	Menin Road
26 September – 3 October	Polygon Wood
4 October	Broodseinde
9 October	Poelcappelle
12, 26 October, 10 November	Passchendaele
20–27 November	Cambrai
20–21 November	Gouzeaucourt

1918

21 March – 5 April	Somme
21–22 March	Fontaine-les-Clercs
21–23 March	St Quentin
23 March	Cugny
24–25 March	Bapaume
26–27 March	Rosières
28 March	Arras
4 April	Avre
5 April	Ancre
9–29 April	Lys
9–11 April	Estaires
10–11 April	Messines
12–25 April	Hazebrouck
13–15 April	Bailleul
17–19 April	Kemmel
18 April	Bethune
22 April	Pecaut Wood
24–25 April	Villers-Bretonneux

25–26 April	Kemmel
29 April	Scherpenberg
27 May – 6 June	Aisne
6 June	Bligny
6 June	Bois des Buttes
4 July	Hamel
20 July – 2 August	Marne
20–31 July	Tardenois
23 July – 2 August	Soissonnais-Ourcq
8–11 August	Amiens
8 August	Harbonnières
21–23 August	Albert
21–23 August	Chuignes
21 August – 5 September	Somme
26 August – 3 September	Arras
26–30 August	Scarpe
29 August	Mont Vidaigne
31 August – 3 September	Bapaume
31 August – 3 September	Mont St Quentin
2–3 September	Drocourt-Quéant
12 September – 9 October	Hindenburg Line
12 September	Havrincourt
18 September	Epehy
27 September – 1 October	Canal du Nord
28 September – 2 October	Ypres
29 September – 2 October	St Quentin Canal
3–6 October	Beaurevoir
8–9 October	Cambrai
14–19 October	Courtrai
17–25 October	Selle
17–18 October	Le Cateau
31 October	Tieghem
1–2 November	Valenciennes
4 November	Sambre
4 November	Le Quesnoy
4–11 November	Pursuit to Mons

ENDNOTES

Chapter 1

1 Gunnar Heinshon, *Shöne und Weltmacht* (Orell Fussli Verlag, 2003)
2 From B.R. Mitchell, *British Historic Statistics* (Cambridge University Press, 1960)
3 Jon Savage, *Teenage – The Creation of Youth 1875–1945* (Chatto and Windus, 2007) p. 154
4 *The Times*, 10 July 1917
5 *The Times*, 18 July 1917
6 Savage, *Teenage*, p. 145
7 Paraphrased from *St John's Daily News*, 10 February 1919 and carried on the 'Newfoundland Grand Banks' website; also in *The Times*, 20 January 1919

Chapter 2

1 George Orwell, *My Country Right or Left* (Harcourt Brace, 1968) p. 589
2 George Orwell, *Collected Essays, Journalism and Letters*, vol I, (Harmondsworth, 1970) p. 528
3 J.M. Winter, *'Propaganda and the Mobilization of Consent'* in Hew Strachan (ed.), *The Oxford Illustrated History of the First World War* (Oxford University Press, 1998) p. 219

4 David Gilmour, *Curzon*, (John Murray, 1994) p. 438
5 From a letter by Thomas Peers now in the Imperial War Museum and quoted by Peter Simkins in *Kitchener's Army* (Pen & Sword Military, 2007) p. 173
6 Facts and figures are from Correlli Barnett, *Britain and Her Army* (Pelican Books, 1974)
7 From J.A. Manghan, *A Noble Specimen of Manhood*, quoted in Jeffrey Richards (ed.), *Imperialism and Juvenile Literature* (Manchester University Press, 1989) p. 180
8 *Ibid.*, pp. 2, 3
9 James Walvin, *A Child's World: A Social History of English Childhood, 1800–1914* (Penguin, 1982) p. 180
10 Quoted in Savage, *Teenage*, p. 90
11 The biographical material, circulation data, and quoted facts are drawn principally from Savage, *Teenage*; Richards (ed.), *Imperialism and Juvenile Literature*; and John M. Mackenzie, *Propaganda and Empire* (Manchester University Press, 1984). The anecdotes about Dr Gordon Stables are taken from 'New Grub Street for Boys', written by Patrick A. Dunae and found in Richards (ed.), *Imperialism and Juvenile Literature*
12 Gyles Brandreth, *I Scream for Ice Cream: Pearls from the Pantomime* (London, 1974) pp. 49–50
13 Mackenzie, *Propaganda and Empire*, pp. 71, 241
14 Savage, *Teenage*, p. 86
15 Mackenzie, *Propaganda and Empire*, p. 155
16 David Gilmour, *The Long Recessional* (John Murray, 2002) p. 161

Chapter 3

1 Winston S. Churchill, *My Early Life, A Roving Commission* (Thornton Butterworth Ltd) p. 246
2 Simkins, *Kitchener's Army*, p. 41
3 John Pollock, *Kitchener* (Constable, 1998) p. 388
4 Michael Carver, *The Boer War* (Sedgwick and Jackson, 1999) p. 252 and Oakes and Parsons, *Old School Ties* (DSN, Peterborough, 2002) p. 26
5 W. Baring Pemberton, *Battles of the Boer War* (Macmillan, 1969) p. 147
6 Thomas Packenham, *The Boer War* (George Weidenfeld & Nicholson Ltd, 1979) p. 252
7 Unless otherwise attributed, the brief summary of the Boer War was paraphrased from Oakes and Parsons, *Old School Ties*. The authors acknowledged their debt and recorded their apologies to Packenham, Carver, Corelli Barnett, James and others

8 Paraphrased from Oakes and Parsons and from Douglas S. Russell, *Winston Churchill Soldier, The Military Life of a Gentleman at War* (Conway, 2005)

9 Carver, *The Boer War*, pp. 138, 139

Chapter 4

1 Quoted in Pollock, *Kitchener*, p. 374

2 Quoted in Gilmour, *Curzon*, p. 447

3 Pollock, *Kitchener*, p. 377

4 Simkins, *Kitchener's New Army*, p. 49, and *The Times,* 7 August 1914

5 Quoted in John Lee, *A Soldier's Life* (Longman, 2000) p. 130

6 '*Report of the War Office Committee of Enquiry into Shell-shock*' (HMSO, London, 1922) p. 175

7 Quoted in Simkins, *Kitchener's New Army*, p. 179

8 Summarised from MacPherson, *War Office Report into Medical Services* (HMSO, 1921)

9 All individual cases from Simkins, *Kitchener's New Army*, p. 183

10 *Labour Leader*, 6 August 1914 (F. Brockway, The Journal of the Independent Labour Party)

11 Rudyard Kipling, *The New Army in Training* (Macmillan and Co. Limited, 1915) pp. 14, 15

12 Field Marshal Lord Carver, *Britain's Army in the Twentieth Century* (Pan Grand Strategy Series in association with the Imperial War Museum, 1998) p. 41

13 Quoted from 'The Shot at Dawn' campaign

14 *The Times*, 4 October 1915

15 *The Times*, 16 October 1915

16 *The Times*, 3 November 1915

Chapter 5

1 Barnett, *Britain and Her Army*, p. 394

2 Simkins, *Kitchener's New Army*, p. 238

3 *Ibid.*, p. 203, quoting an unpublished account by Patterson held in the Imperial War Museum

4 All quotes, unless otherwise stated, are from James Norman Hall, *Kitchener's Mob – Adventures of an American in the British Army* (Haughton Mifflin Company, 1916)

5 The Junger quote comes from E. Junger, *The Storm of Steel* (Constable, 1994) quoted in Savage, *Teenage*, p. 150

6 CK to Mrs Balestier, 28 October 1914, Dunham Papers, quoted in Gilmour, *The Long Recessional*, p. 257

7 Simkins, *Kitchener's New Army*, pp. 179–80

8 Quotes from John Kipling's letters to his father come from '*Times Online*' and are contained in Elliot L. Gilbert (ed.), *O Beloved Kids* (Max Press, 2007)

9 Quoted from the Kipling Papers by Charles Carrington in *Rudyard Kipling – His Life and Works* (Penguin, 1986) p. 509

10 Carrington, *Kipling*, p. 510

11 Quoted by Dorothea Flothow, The Kipling Journal, vol. 82, April 2008

12 Gilmour, *The Long Recessional*, p. 257

Chapter 6

1 *Reading School Magazine*, July 1914, p. 224

2 I am grateful to David Snape, who researched the life of William Eppstein for me

3 Savage, *Teenage*, p. 104

4 Mackenzie, *Propaganda and Empire*, p. 214

5 J.A. Mangan, 'Images of Empire in the late Victorian public school', *Journal of Educational Administration and History*, XII, 1 January 1980, p. 31. Quoted in Mackenzie, *Propaganda and Empire*, p. 248

6 Unless otherwise stated this chapter is drawn from Oakes and Parsons, *Old School Ties* and *Reading School – the First 800 Years*.

Chapter 7

1 Victor Bonham-Carter, 'Wully Robertson' in Alistair Horne (ed.), *Telling Lives* (Macmillan, 2003) p. 181

2 Barnett, *Britain and Her Army*, p. 374

3 Oakes and Parsons, *Old School Ties*, p. 177

4 All the above is by kind permission of the Queen's Royal Surrey Regiment Association and of Lt. Colonel Leslie Wilson who supplied the information in private correspondence and on the regimental website

5 Commemorated at Poperinge New Military Cemetery, West Vlaanderen, Belgium; www.clerkehome58.freeserve.co.uk

6 There has been no judicial execution in the UK since 1964 and capital punishment, civilian and military, has been outlawed by the Human Rights Act since 1998

7 David Englander, 'Mutinies and Military Morale' in Strachan (ed.), *The Oxford Illustrated History of the First World War*, p. 192

8 Paraphrased from HRH the Duke of Kent, President of the Commonwealth War Graves Commission (www.cwmg.org)

9 Oakes and Parsons, *Old School Ties*, p. 253

10 From Hall, *Kitchener's Mob*, p. 42

11 From a facsimile shown at www.cwgc.co.uk

12 See www.cwgc.co.uk

13 See www.cwgc.co.uk and others

14 *Waterford News and Star*, 7 November 2003

Chapter 8

1 H.W.Wilson (ed.), *The Great War*, vol. 12 (The Amalgamated Press, London, 1914–1918) and Gary Mead, *The Good Soldier – The Biography of Douglas Haig*, p. 341

2 Wilson (ed.), *The Great War*, vol. 13, p. 307

3 *Ibid.*, p. 332

4 Ernest Glaeser, *Class of 1902* (Viking, 1929), quoted in Savage, *Teenage*, p. 183

5 Quoted in Savage, *Teenage*, p. 182

6 Richard Percival Graves, *Oxford Dictionary of National Biography* (Oxford University Press, www.Oxforddnb.com)

7 Unless otherwise stated, this and subsequent remarks about shell-shock, its symptoms and cure are summarised from G.E. Smith, *Shell-Shock and its Lessons* (Manchester University Press, 1917) and W.H.R. Rivers MD, 'The Repression of War Experience', a paper delivered before the Section of Psychiatry, Royal Society of Medicine, 4 December 1917

8 Mead, *The Good Soldier*, pp. 362, 363

9 Adrian Gregory, *Silence of Memory* (Berg, 1994) p. 29

10 Quoted by Jane Shilling in *The Times*, 6 June 2008

SELECT BIBLIOGRAPHY

Barnett, Corelli, *Britain and her Armies 1509–1970* (Pelican Books, 1974)

Brett, Rachel and Specht, Irma, *Young Soldiers – Why they Choose to Fight* (Lynne Rienner Publishing, Boulder, Colorado, 2004)

Carrington, Charles, *Rudyard Kipling: His Life and Work* (Penguin, 1972)

Carver, Michael, *Field Marshall: Britain and her Armies in the Twentieth Century* (Macmillan, 1998)

Carver, Michael, *The Boer War* (Sedgwick and Jackson, 1999)

Cockerill, A.W., *Sons of the Brave – The Story of Boy Soldiers* (Leo Cooper in association with Martin, Secker and Warburg Ltd, 1984)

Gilmour, David, *Curzon* (John Murray, 1994)

——, *The Long Recessional* (John Murray, 2002)

Hill, James Norman, *Kitchener's Mob – Adventures of an American in the British Army* (Houghton Mifflin Company, Boston and New York, 1916)

Kipling, Rudyard, *The New Army in Training* (Macmillan and Co., 1915)

Lee, John, *A Soldier's Life – General Sir Ian Hamilton 1853–1947* (Pan Books)

Lloyd, Trevor, *Empire – The History of the British Empire* (Hambledon and London, 2001)

Mackenzie, John M., *Propaganda and Empire – The Manipulation of British Public Opinion, 1880–1960* (Manchester University Press, Manchester and New York, 1984)

Mead, Gary, *The Good Soldier – The Biography of Douglas Haig* (Atlantic Books, 2007)

Oakes, John and Parsons, Martin, *Old School Ties* (DSM, Peterborough, 2003)

———, *et al.*, *Reading School – The First 800 Years* (DSM, Peterborough, 2005)

Packenham, Thomas, *The Boer War* (George Weidenfeld & Nicholson Ltd, 1979)

Pollock, John, *Kitchener* (Constable, 1998)

Richards, Jeffrey (ed.), *Imperialism and Juvenile Literature* (Manchester University Press, 1989)

Russell, Douglas S., *Winston Churchill – Soldier* (Conway, 2005)

Savage, Jon, *Teenage – The Creation of Youth 1875–1945* (Chatto and Windus, 2007)

Simkins, Peter, *Kitchener's Army – The Raising of the New Armies 1914–1916* (Pen and Sword Military, 2007)

Smith, Michael, *Kipling's Sussex* (Brownleaf, 2008)

Strachan, Huw (ed.), *The Oxford Illustrated History of the First World War* (Oxford University Press, 1998)

Van Emden, Richard, *Boy Soldiers of the Great War* (Headline, 2005)

Wilson, H.W. (ed.), *The Great War – The Standard History of the All-Europe Conflict*, 12 Volumes (The Amalgamated Press, London, 1914–1919)

Archives

The Commonwealth War Graves Commission, *Debt of Honour*

The Kendrick Boys' School Magazines, 1909–1915

The Old Redingensians Archive

The Reading School Archive and Magazine Library

The Times Archive, London

INDEX

Ranks and titles, as far as possible, reflect the career best of those named in the index. Abbreviations used: Pte – Private; Cpl – Corporal; Sgt – Sergeant; Lt – Lieutenant; Lt Col – Lieutenant Colonel; Maj Gen – Major General; Lt Gen – Lieutenant General